MORE PRAISE FOR *GOD in the Sink...*

Around 14 years ago, I began receiving *Notes From Toad Hall*... Since then, I've saved every issue, devoting an entire shelf in my office to their preservation. With *God in the Sink*, I'm thrilled to have an essay collection that ranges through the three plus decades that *Notes* has been gracing the mailboxes of grateful readers. There's so much I had missed and now all this gold is in one book! As one essay turns to another, we're invited to see that it's in the daily, ordinary, hard, lovely, and real places of our lives that God is with us and for us, even at the kitchen sink.

Andi Ashworth
Author of Real Love for Real Life: The Art
and Work of Caring
Editor-in-Chief of the Art House America Blog

Funny, painful, honest. She seems to believe that God is ready to welcome us in the most unlikely of places no matter who we are or where we've been. I am grateful for this belief. By it we rediscover Jesus, present with grace amid the dignity of broken persons, the complexity of human circumstances, and the common joys and errors of family, work, and love. The result is a renewed and palpable sense that our deepest longings for home have a hearing. And that the way home is surpassingly found among "the pleasures and hopes of small matters." Read this book and you will discover a wise companion traveling with you into the adventure that each day brings.

Zack Eswine
Pastor of Riverside Presbyterian Church
Author of Sensing Jesus *and* Preaching
to a Post-Everything World

As a mom of three really active boys, a pastor's wife with a "creative" edge (i.e.: I can't focus on much of one thing for very long) *Notes* was/is always a breath of fresh air for me. It was mostly just for me — not just an excerpt in one of my husband's magazines — I could finish an article with a cup of tea... steal away in a corner of the house or yard where nobody could find me for a few precious moments... and in those pages I found encouragement. Many times God worked through your stories to encourage me to press on as a woman of faith. Thank you, Margie, for following your calling so beautifully!

Gwendylyn Sembler
Cedar Grove, WI

In this wonderfully honest, raw, and joyful book, Margie Haack's words convey a whisper of sanity and authenticity in the midst of an otherwise clamorous world. May we all learn and grow from the window she has provided us into the life of faith.

David Richter
Lead Minister, Christ the King
Church, Somerville, MA

Reading Margie Haack is at one and the same time deeply satisfying, because we are sure she knows us, and horribly troubling, because she knows us. Like her, we are people trying hard to keep going, aware — as she writes in her new book, *God in the Sink* — that "the rhythm of ordinary life is rarely that exciting or sensational for all who wander the wastelands of earth." Whether we enter into her world in the quiet of our own hearts, or in the company of family and friends, her words are a gift of grace, allowing us to remember to remember what matters most-- and to imagine that it is possible to still love what is ours to love, wounded people in a wounded world that we are.

Steve Garber
Director of The Washington Institute for Faith,
Vocation, & Culture
Author of The Fabric of Faithfulness
and Visions of Vocation

I've been addicted to Margie Haack's newsletter, *Notes from Toad Hall*, since 1997. I think it began with something about carpenter ants ("Why do I write such drivel to busy people who need to be reading about important things? Well, it is because this is where most of us live the better portion of our lives. Right here in the vast, ordinary, wasteland of our days. It is a place where God is often unacknowledged in a million little disasters and events. It is the place of broken appliances and unexpected inconveniences") which made me understand that this was no mamby-pamby Christian writer. Here was someone who connected the broadness and the depth and the fabulous wackiness of God with that same stuff in life. She's refreshingly nuts, and is in the dirt with us, but she writes better than anyone does about that dirt. Margie has helped me grapple with the light and the dark, the confusion and the dancing that makes up figuring out how to live as a Christian. I know she talks about being influenced by Ann Lamott, but when I started reading Ann Lamott, I thought she sounded so much like Margie.

God in the Sink puts some of my favorite pieces together to enjoy again.

Leslie Van Orsdel
Manager: Sales Engagement, Key Accounts &
Operations at Bloomberg Government, NYC

God is so great, nothing is outside of His control; He is so intimate, no detail of our lives escapes His involvement. Margie's latest book is an invitation into the ordinariness of life where we learn over and over again Christ is in all things — even a sink full of dirty dishes. If God seems absent from the commonplace of your life, Margie will help open your eyes to see Him more. In her latest book, *God in the Sink*, Margie invites us into the common-ness of life. But there is no boredom here. Instead, we are repeatedly confronted with the hidden glory of Christ in the most surprising of places. The One who made all things and is in all things, is also present in the dailyness of our lives. Margie has been given the eyes to reveal Him to us.

Ed Hague
Founder, Macpro Services, Tallahassee, FL

Margie Haack has long been one of my favorite writers. Her occasional essays (which are sometimes as intimate as confessions, as brazen as a stand-up comedian, as glorious about the spirituality of the ordinary as a modern mystic) have come into our home for years in her wonderful *Notes from Toad Hall*. That the best of these candid, entertaining, excellently-crafted pieces are now collected and offered in this lovely volume is truly a great thing. Or in the toothpaste tube recaptured from the toilet bowl. Or in one's own crankiness and fear and pain. Get this book, enjoy these writings, and learn from this unusually transparent wife, mother, grandmother, steward of Toad Hall, daughter of grace, plucky follower of Christ — and very, very talented author.

Byron Borger
Owner, Hearts & Minds Books

In this humorous and vulnerable collection of stories, Margie opens the shades of her home, Toad Hall, and invites us to see that in all stages and seasons of life, God is eager to fill even our most mundane moments with meaning and grace. As a fellow wife, mother, and chronic fixer of the world's problems, I saw glimpses of myself in her efforts to be a faithful follower of Jesus in the smallest of things: feeding her family, welcoming in strangers, or losing her car in a parking lot while attempting to save the world. In her stories, we see that God is in the floorboards and in our failures, in the stairways and in our successes, and is truly Lord over even the dirtiest dishes in the sink and in our souls. This is a deeply encouraging book.

Elizabeth Berget
Author of the blog Carpé Season

God in
the Sink

God in the Sink

Essays from Toad Hall

by Margie L. Haack

Walk in love,
Margie Haack

God in the Sink: Essays from Toad Hall

Published by:

Doulos Resources, PO Box 69485, Oro Valley, AZ 85737; PHONE: (901) 201-4612 WEB-SITE: www.doulosresources.org.

℗ Copyright 2014 Margie L. Haack. Some rights reserved. This work is licensed under the Creative Commons Attribution-NonCommercial-NoDerivs License. To view a copy of this license, (a) visit www.creativecommons.org; or, (b) send a letter to Creative Commons, 171 2nd Street, Suite 300, San Francisco, California, 94105, USA.

Cover and interior design by J.E. Eubanks, Jr., 2014.

Please address all questions about rights and reproduction to Doulos Resources: PHONE: (901) 201-4612; E-MAIL: info@doulosresources.org.

All scripture quotations, unless otherwise indicated, are taken from the Holy Bible, New International Version®, NIV®. Copyright ©1973, 1978, 1984, 2011 by Biblica, Inc.™ Used by permission of Zondervan. All rights reserved worldwide. www.zondervan.com The "NIV" and "New International Version" are trademarks registered in the United States Patent and Trademark Office by Biblica, Inc.™

Published 2014

Printed in the United States of America by Ingram/Lightning Source

This book is printed using archival paper that is produced according to Sustainable Forestry Initiative® (SFI®) Certified Sourcing.

Haack, Margie L., 1946–

God in the Sink: Essays from Toad Hall.

ISBNs: 978-1-937063-63-4 (print); 978-1-937063-62-7 (digital)

2014950975

13 14 15 16 17 18 19 20   10 9 8 7 6 5 4 3 2 1

DEDICATED TO THE MEMORY of Edith Schaeffer (1914 –2013), whose life and rambling Family Letters inspired my own.

Contents

ARRIVING WITHIN SIGHT OF his old home, he rested on his oars and surveyed the land cautiously. All seemed very peaceful and deserted and quiet. He could see the whole front of Toad Hall, glowing in the evening sunshine, the pigeons settling by twos and threes along the straight line of the roof; the garden, a blaze of flowers; the creek that led up to the boathouse, the little wooden bridge that crossed it; all tranquil, uninhabited, apparently waiting for his return.

(from *The Wind in the Willows* by Kenneth Grahame)

God in the Sink
Spring 2014

"What is God doing in the sink?"

My granddaughter, Ava Lou, was standing on a stool washing dishes with a sink full of cold water and soapsuds as only a four-year-old can "wash" dishes. She was looking at bobblehead Jesus who was overseeing the process.

I wondered how to explain irony to her. How to say it had an obscure, but special meaning to me. I've often thought, I should put it away because people must look at it all the time and wonder if I'm a heretic of some kind, worshiping saints or idols or something equally suspicious. This is my explanation. He was a gift from a friend, Jeremy Huggins. Together we appreciate the humor and irony in Christian paraphernalia that is marketed in certain stores. Things like Frisbees that say "Flying high for Jesus." Or night-lights with the inscription: "Jesus is the light of the world."

So there Jesus sits bobbling on the edge of my sink as a reminder to laugh at ourselves for the absurd ways in which we represent

Christian faith to the world, and to try to push against the trivialization of such great a thing as the gospel. I mean no disrespect to a God I love. I think he knows that.

When it took too long to think of a simple answer to this dear child, she moved on to the next question.

"Can I give God a bath? He wants a bath." I gently said no. He will get all rusty inside and not bobble anymore, so I quickly moved to pack him in a box, ready for my next kitchen. Yes, *my next kitchen.* The words were both exhilarating and terrifying.

Ava Lou and her mother (Micah, my daughter-in-law) were visiting for three days to help us clean out Toad Hall's attic. Our attic of 33 years. Micah's presence and and help was stabilizing. I was thankful she was a runner because there must have been a million trips up and down the stairs. It was accomplished in record time because I was determined to be ruthless. Everything down and out. Throw away, give to family, give to charity, sell if possible. Label what to keep and where it should go in the next place. Done!

WHEN WE ARRIVED AT this house 33 years ago, our youngest child was three years old. Our children were awestruck when we pulled up to the curb for the very first time and looked up at our new home. Our oldest daughter, who had just turned 12, exclaimed, "Why, this must be exactly like Toad Hall!" (from a favorite childhood book, *The Wind in the Willows*). They had never seen such imposing three-story homes with dormers and enormous front porches. They had only known low, one-story adobes that rambled along in the hot New Mexico sun. To them, an American Gothic Foursquare looked amazingly like a mansion, possibly even as great a house as *Toad Hall.* So that's what it became, christened by our children: "Toad Hall."

What began as our ministry newsletter for Ransom Fellowship in 1982 soon became *Notes From Toad Hall.* It was our desire to update

2

the friends on our mailing list in a way that was informative but not so dull you would want your time back after you read it. The challenge was how to write truthfully about the place where we all must dwell — in whatever is our ordinary and everyday — without over-emphasizing what our culture, Christians included, defines as success. The rhythm of ordinary life is rarely that exciting or sensational. I wanted to honestly share what it meant to be a faithful follower of Jesus not so much when a hundred people praised my spinach quiche and artisan bread or a lecture on tattoos – that part was easy – it has always been much harder for me to believe God calls us to the very place where the thistles and thorns of the fallen world creep into our vocations and callings every day. It's a place where there are painful disagreements with your spouse, where a child's vomit stains the woodwork, and where the espresso machine explodes. Faithfulness is tested and strained through the mundane, often boring, offices of life where the pantry must be kept stocked and mistakes are made when filing your taxes. These things are so ordinary we hardly consider that this is where God mentors us and gives us grace and rest and meaning and life, but these were the bones that grew into a personal essay I included in every letter. This is a collection of some of those essays gathered together with the hope that others would be encouraged, as I have been, to recognize God's presence in the ordinary circumstances of our lives.

So life continues to be a demonstration of God in the sink with us — he has been with us through all stages of life, appearing in the unexpected joys of fireflies in summer and snowmen in winter, and mixing it up with the human struggles common to us all. And now, Jesus watches over us in the midst of boxes and the screech of packing tape, helping us move on to a new stage after so many years in one place.

God in the Sink

THERE WERE REASONS TO move from this hundred-year-old Midwestern home. We needed to leave before the decision was made for us. All our bedrooms were on the second floor. There was only a half-bath on the main floor. Our neighborhood was increasing in noise and traffic. (As writers, we value quiet.) With many of our closest friends having moved away, there was less community. We knew that the longer we stayed the harder it would be to say goodbye to a place where we lived more than half our lives. Frankly, old people can get calcified and stubborn.

We've been in our new home for a month, and today I am sitting in my office looking out the window. About five feet away a little flycatcher hops down an oak limb looking for insects. The sun is sending rays through the canopy into the ravine below. It lights leafy corridors with a hundred hues of green. We are 85 percent moved in. Denis says it is 85 percent. I don't know why 85. But I know there are many fewer boxes. The ones that remain will be okay as we find new spaces for their contents.

Bobblehead Jesus has a new sink to oversee. God made it to our new home. As if I didn't think he would come? Every morning as I reach into the cabinet and pull out my coffee mug, I'm reminded that just as he watched over Toad Hall every moment of my life down through the years, he will bless this place and the people who dwell here as only he can.

Touching a Stranger
Winter 2008

"*I* don't think I've met you. My name is Margie."

I said this as I held out my hand, warm and friendly, to a young woman standing in the foyer after church.

It's possible for someone to attend for quite awhile and I might not recognize her face. That's easy even in our relatively small church. We're out of town. They're out of town or working. Add a little weekend sickness, and there's a chance you might not notice a new person for weeks, maybe years. So even if I suspect I've seen them before I never ask, "Are you new to Trinity?" I'm conscientiously neutral so we can give each other an out. "I don't think I've met you." "I've been in India." "I need cataract surgery."

Anyways, it's risky — the whole business of introducing yourself to a stranger; when I force myself to do it, I think I deserve a little pat from God saying, "Nicely done, Margie. I know meeting strangers is hard. Your memory is bad. You are 50% introvert, but you need to pay better attention. Focus. (Her name is Heather. Heather.) I know you'd like to just go home, fix an omelet and watch the Vikings lose, still, you reached out to someone who needed a warm greeting. Enter into paradise." I imagine that person will be really grateful for this small gesture and perhaps it will be the beginning of more. Who knows?

None of this happened with the above nice, young woman. She looked me in the eye and said, "Well. We have met before."

(I'm thinking. Okay. Yes. That's entirely possible. However, for forgetting your face, I'll make it up to you by being utterly charming here.)

"In fact," she went on, "I stayed at your house last year."

You know how comedians sometimes use the bass drum, snare, and cymbals to deliver a single, syncopated beat? Ka-ta-boom. I heard it there in the church foyer, and it drowned everything and so completely derailed my concentration that when she did tell me her name, I still didn't get it. Are you familiar with the Bunny Suicides calendar I'm so fond of? I thought of several bunny ways to off myself, like tying a grenade to a boomerang. Ah, well.

So much for the meaningful practice of hospitality. So much for years of reading about and modeling "I was a stranger and you took me in." I can't even remember someone who stayed in our home less than a year ago. (There was a little more to the story, but later.)

Feeling like an idiot is pretty familiar territory and I've learned to quickly move on — or write about it. Being confronted with one's limitations and failures isn't such a bad thing. Jung liked to point out we learn nothing from our successes and everything from our mistakes, not that I base my entire life on what Jung says. Christine Pohl clears it up further when she writes, "Humility is a crucial virtue for hospitality, and especially important in keeping hosts' power in check. Power is a complicated dimension of hospitality" (*Making Room* by C.D. Pohl, p. 120). If this is true, my power meter registers zero, so perhaps there is hope, after all.

Who Knows What Risk?

As CHRISTIANS, WE'RE CALLED to practice a rhythm of hospitality at all times and in all stages of life. We practice it not because we're perfect in caring for others or because we never stumble in remembering the details of another's life or are wealthy or have a lot of free time. We invite the stranger into our lives because we answer Christ who calls to us through them saying, "I was hungry and you gave me something to eat, I was thirsty and you gave me something to drink, I was a stranger and you invited me in" (Matt. 25:35).

Moving out of the safety of private orderly lives, we meet him in the lives of the marginalized, poor, and fatherless. The fatherlessness part of the equation interests me as my own father was killed in an accident leaving my 17-year-old mother with no means of support. Currently living in the postmodern age, we can expand the fatherless category to include the person whose father is alive but has abandoned the family. Or he may be a father who is there but too busy with his own life to be engaged in the lives of his children. We must be aware that many we meet don't carry their hunger on the surface of their lives, rather, they remain buried under layers of enculturated behavior that require gentleness and time to peel back.

Over the years Denis and I have invited many people into our lives, and as I approach an older stage of life, time allows me to look back and pontificate about this practice of touching the stranger in our midst. Sometimes our encounters were brief and soon forgotten — like the young woman above. (After that Sunday in the foyer I learned she had visited Paige who at the time was renting our studio apartment behind Toad Hall. Paige brought her over to meet us one evening, and I had utterly forgotten about this.) There have been times when it seemed whatever we did was wrong or not enough, or made no difference at all. Not knowing the outcome of our efforts, we may be tempted to ask, "Will the interruption to my life be worth it? Is this person deserving of my sacrifice? Does he know I should be fixing the leak in my roof rather than hearing about what shenanigans his teenage daughter is up to? And what if my drain gets matted and clogged with creepy stuff when they shower, or the pages are turned down in my favorite book, or the drill is never returned all because I got involved?"

When we engage a stranger, we can't know the risk involved, nor should we make it our goal to see long-term effects of our hospitality. The early church fathers viewed acts of hospitality toward others as if they were the welcoming acts performed for the incarnate Lord. Long before modern humanitarian relief efforts, Augustine argued directly against the tendency to gauge the worthiness of any particular person by saying, "We are not to search out only those we consider worthy, in case the worthy might be excluded. You cannot be a judge and sifter of hearts." (*The Good Works Reader* by Thomas Oden) Augustine goes on to teach that the reason our giving should not be based upon moral worth is because we ourselves were taken in by Christ when we were dark and broken. We receive strangers because, in doing so, we are loving Christ as he has loved us. Sometimes when we get to know a stranger over a period of time, that person who first came to us in need becomes a friend who gives back many times over.

A Thousand Reckless Ways

THE DIFFICULTIES AND JOYS of hospitality are often closely intertwined and the following illustrates both unexpected blessing and the struggle with human limitations when we encounter strangers.

When Denis answered the door a slender young woman with blue eyes and straight blond hair down to her waist stood on the steps clutching a worn backpack. Denis called me to come to the door, because she was asking to stay with us, and we had a policy of "no crashers." I picked up our one-year-old daughter and carried her with me to the front door. Denis introduced me, "This is Nancy. She's asking to stay with us."

"But we're not a crash pad." I said it with a note of accusation. It was 1971 and there were still plenty of disenchanted hitchhikers crossing the country searching for a place to drop acid and find the "Stairway To Heaven." I was annoyed that Denis hadn't just sent her away. The four young men already living with us were funny and charming, but their all-night jamming sessions and the amount of food they consumed was taxing my patience and destroying our budget. At the time we were working with a large assortment of newly converted or spiritually searching young people. We called our home "His House" which, at the time sounded more evocative. Our living room was open forum every night for live music, discussion, prayer, and coffee, but we had to have *some* limits.

"My dad dropped me off over there," she pointed to the Piggly Wiggly parking lot across the street from where we lived "and I told him I'd be staying here. He's gone back to Las Cruces." She looked at us. "Please? I heard you were Christians, sort of like L'Abri, and that you took people in."

She was barely 20 and spoke with an appealing little lisp. There was vulnerability about her and it seemed uncaring and dangerous to be simply dump your daughter off in the middle of our run-down neighborhood in Albuquerque. We looked at each other and a slight nod passed between Denis and me.

"You can come in and stay the night, but I'm not sure about after that. We don't have a bed for you, but we have extra blankets and there is the floor."

Her face brightened, and she entered our home and claimed a corner of the living room. That night, when Denis led a Bible study

discussion, it was crowded as usual, and Nancy made some preco-
cious, insightful comments — enough to swivel my head and capture
our full attention. Late that night after everyone left she told Denis he
needed to read more of Francis Schaeffer. And she was happy to tell
him exactly why. We learned she was a new Christian and had just
come back from a place called Swiss L'Abri.

She stayed the next day and the next, and that summer became
the first of several summers she spent in our home as part of our
family. We've loved her ever since. In 2005 Nancy Randolph Pearcey's
book *Total Truth: Liberating Christianity from Its Cultural Captivity* won the
Gold Medallion Award for best book of the year.

THE SAME SUMMER WE met Nancy, Kathy Barboa found us — or maybe we found her because I don't remember the first time we met her
either.

Kathy had been on heroin and living on the street for a year
when Teen Challenge took her in and taught her something about
the power of the Gospel. She made a profession of faith and really
wanted a new life. She was 15 when she moved in with us.

Kathy had wealthy parents, but they grew weary of her troubled life and kicked her out; she talked some about their detachment.
When he was home, her father sat behind the newspaper never looking up, not answering or engaging her when she talked to him. To
get her mother's attention she dropped syringes and needles in the
hallway and on the front steps, hoping her mom would find them and
be alarmed. But her mother never mentioned them.

Over the Rhine has a song titled "All I need is Everything" in which
they sing, "Inside, outside, feel new skin / all I need is everything /
feel the slip and the grip of grace again…" (From the CD *Good Dog,
Bad Dog,* 2000) Certainly it's true that at the end of the day we *all*
need that "Everything." But I sensed this acutely with Kathy. She

was so wounded she needed *rock bottom* everything. And what did we have to offer? Not much. We were young and poor and pretty naïve about some things.

One night as I sat on Kathy's bed saying good night, we talked about little things, nothing profound, and suddenly she began sobbing and couldn't stop. My sitting there so casually, tenderly, almost absently touching her was something her mom had never done. Just this ordinary thing undid her.

We loved her, but not perfectly. She was a huge trial for us, combining little girl needs with sexy street-wise attitude. Sometimes she was very exasperating. In the end she left us because she couldn't stay off drugs or away from the men who used her. We told ourselves, it wasn't our fault, but I always wondered, had we done enough? For four years we heard from her, sometimes in the middle of the night crying, wanting us to pray, needing us to come pick her up from some dump. She wanted life to be different, but she never overcame her terrifying addictions.

Then one day as I prepared dinner listening to the news with half an ear, I heard an item that made me drop the dish I was holding; "Today a young woman, Kathy Barboa, has been shot to death by an ex-boyfriend in what looks like a lover's quarrel. Police are investigating…" I turned to look at the television screen and saw Kathy's body lying on the sidewalk in a pool of blood covered by a sheet.

So had she been ushered into heaven that day? I thought so. All her wounds would have been healed by the time of the newscast — all the brokenness we could not fix. I saw her as fresh and virgin in a way that wasn't possible here on earth. Jesus would have already killed her blues forever. Someday, I'm going to be so glad to see her again and laugh about the way she sometimes shocked me.

WE PLAY SMALL PARTS in the lives of many people we encounter.

Hospitality is practiced in a thousand reckless little ways. We don't know what will be the outcome of caring for the stranger. God is under no obligation to tell us, and yet he notices and controls the consequences of each little temporal act, and they will not go unrewarded.

A Postscript on being Home

We lie in our beds in the dark. There is a picture of the children on the bureau. A patch of moonlight catches our clothes thrown over the back of a chair. We can hear the faint rumble of the furnace in the cellar. We are surrounded by the reassurance of the familiar. When the weather is bad, we have shelter. When things are bad in our lives, we have a place where we can retreat to lick our wounds while tens of thousands of people, many of them children, wander the dark streets in search of some corner to lie down in out of the wind.

Yet we are homeless even so in the sense of having homes but not being really at home in them. To be really at home is to be really at peace, and there can be no real peace for any of us until there is some measure of real peace for all of us. When we close our eyes to the deep needs of other people whether they live on the streets or under our own roof — and when we close our eyes to our own deep need to reach out to them – we can never be fully at home anywhere.

(*Wishful Thinking: A Seeker's ABC*, Frederick Buechner, p. 46)

IN THIS LIFE WE are blessed if we have moments of tasting, of small knowings when we're on to something very like home. We long for it to be permanent, not just for ourselves but for all who wander the wastelands of earth. The words of Christ are sweet when he assures us: "Let not your heart be troubled. Trust in God; trust also in me. In my Father's house are many rooms; if it were not so, I would have told you. I'm going there to prepare a place for you" (John 14:1–2).

As we wait for the "already, but not yet" it is our privilege to share the fragrance of that Home that is coming with those who pass by.

Thunderstorms & Angels
JULY 1981

EVERYTHING WE OWNED WAS strewn throughout the first and second floors of the house. Boxes teetered in stacks halfway to the 10-foot ceilings, black plastic garbage bags spilled pillows and blankets, paintings and artwork wrapped in old sheets were stacked on radiators. The three people we knew in Rochester who had helped unload the truck were gone. The rental truck was returned; we were alone.

Our beds weren't set up, but I was determined to find clean pajamas for the kids among the litter of the bedrooms. Despite having carefully labeled every box we packed in Albuquerque, I gave up that search and began digging through stuffed animals, clothing and blankets. *Now* all I wanted was a bath towel so I could shower. Everyone was crabby and starving. I waded through wads of newspaper on the kitchen floor. It was past suppertime and I now understood why spider mothers eat their young. At one time there had been food in our cooler, but three days of travel made what was left so revolting only a raccoon would have been interested.

In the southwest, purple-black clouds with a greenish tinge were mounting up over St. Mary's hospital and the giant elm trees lining the boulevards were unnaturally still. Not a leaf turned. We felt faint rumbles like a distant war was being fought just beyond the horizon. No one wanted to stay home alone in a strange house with an attic door just off the upstairs hall and a basement with a cistern while Mother went in search of food. Staying together seemed wise.

After what seemed like days of carrot sticks and apple slices, Denis wanted meat. We thought we'd seen a cheap steakhouse nearby, but we couldn't remember where. With Jerem and Sember crying with exhaustion and Marsena trying not to, we piled into our Volkswagon van and finally stopped at a pay phone to see if we could find an address in a phone book. We were too tired remember the names of any cheap, chain steakhouses we had ever known. Anywhere. Anywhere on the continent. Or the world. We could only think of "The Bonanza Sirloin Pit." The restaurant pages were torn from phone book and I was beginning to cry, too.

Out of sheer desperation Denis dialed "0." This was back when phone companies and information personnel were live and local and a telephone operator actually came on the line to ask how they could help. Denis explained we had just moved to Rochester and didn't know where anything was and was there a Sirloin Stockade or something like it; just an address would help. She first asked where we were. Not understanding, Denis said, Rochester, Minnesota. No, she repeated, *where* are you, as in what street are you standing on?

Denis climbed back in the van, pale and trembling. She not only told him what restaurant we should try, she told him exactly how to get there and informed him it was about three blocks from where he was standing. We were stunned. Could she be an angel? We had never heard of such a thing.

Marsena asked why I was crying. I felt childish, ridiculous, but I couldn't stop saying, thank you God, thank you God, we were so hungry and so tired and you sent a telephone operator to help us!

~

By the time we got back to our new home it was storming. Rain sheeted the windows and torrents of water swirled through the streets. No one wanted to sleep alone in a strange, new house. No way was Jerem going to lie down in a room with stacked with shadowy boxes and lumpy shapes ready to spring to life in the dark; he'd always had an active nighttime imagination. We found sheets and blankets, shoved aside the boxes in the largest bedroom, and made beds on the floor. We had just arranged our bodies and turned off the light when a flash so intense it momentarily blinded us lit the room. There was no time to count "Mississippi one, Mississippi two" to estimate out how far away the lightening struck. The instantaneous concussion crashed through our chests and shook the house to its stone foundation. It was surely worthy of the 101st Airborne dropping a thousand bombs.

In the darkness that followed we laughed nervously, and all the more as we heard the howling of the civil defense sirens, first from the west and then from the north as they went off all over town. Cuddling together, we prayed thanking God for a dry home, kind people who helped us carry all our things inside before the rain, and a telephone operator who helped us find some supper and asked him to keep us safe. We had so forgotten tornado weather rules, we didn't even think of rushing our family to the safety of the basement.

The next morning sunlight sparkled through leaded glass windows while we found milk and cold cereal for breakfast. That's when the sirens began sounding again and again. We pulled a radio from a box and turned to a local station to see if there was some cause for alarm and learned they were warning of flash flooding as the creeks and rivers overflowed their banks from the seven inches of rain that fell during the night — another reminder of how far we were from the high and dry deserts of New Mexico where seven inches of rain was almost the annual rainfall.

IT DIDN'T TAKE LONG to unpack our belongings into this solid gothic foursquare built in 1916. The amount of storage space in the garage, the dusty walk-up attic and basement put me in a rapturous coma. Unbelievable coming from a small home where every closet and shelf bulged! The honey-colored hardwood floors, the wide oak trim and six panel doors gave the rooms a solidity that could surely withstand floods and tornados and soothe the worst family quarrels. Lovely touches here and there — high ceilings, leaded glass windows, and a screened-in back porch.

There is no doubt Minnesotans have an accent. This is where I grew up, but my ear could not hear it until I had lived in New Mexico for 12 years. I had forgotten how often they say, "Ya, sure," or end their sentences with a preposition. Now that I'm back, that sing-songy way of speaking and the elongated vowels slip easily off my native tongue, as if it had never left. I think we're home.

The Case of
the Missing Binoculars
DECEMBER 1987

*H*ISTORICALLY, I THINK THE most sorrowful prayer for deliverance must have been spoken by Jesus as he prayed it in the garden on the eve of his arrest: "O my Father, if it be possible, let this cup pass from me; nevertheless not as I will, but yours be done" (Matt. 26:39). Following the example of the psalmist and many fathers and mothers from history, we cry out with our own prayers for deliverance. We pray for things large and small and don't always know; whether this cup will "pass from me," or with God's help will I need to drink it?

Sometimes God grants answers to a prayer in the most singular way, like in the case of our son Jerem. I would like to say he was lucky, but since I'm mostly a Calvinist, I better give credit to providence.

It seems to me that God pays special attention to the hearts of children, kindly hearing them and pouring grace on them. I've known quite a few who have prayed a childish prayer and been answered in such a miraculous way that it became part of the evidence that points toward his existence, rather like looking at the stars in the night sky and thinking there must be a creator.

There was a boy I knew in junior high, who hasn't made a profession of faith so far as I know. I've heard he concedes there is a God though he's not interested in all that right now. He remembers when he was a little boy how much he loved butterflies, animals, and flowers. (He grew up to be a veterinarian.) Most of all he loved birds: how they flew, gracefully swooping from barn roof to the ground, how their songs carried across the land, how their colors flashed through the leaves. One warm day as he walked along a field of sweet clover, he watched the tiny gold finches dipping along the fence line to feed on thistle heads. He longed to hold one of these exquisite little birds. So he prayed aloud, "God, if there is a God, you could make a bird sit on my hand, and I will believe in you." He no sooner said the words, held out his hand, and a bright yellow goldfinch perched on his finger and sang to him.

On the day I am remembering, Jerem's prayer was a prayer for deliverance from me: "God, please rescue me from my mom's anger. Please, please help me find those binoculars."

What precipitated this was that I noticed Denis' binoculars – a birthday gift from me — were missing. I knew right well who'd taken them and went straight to Jerem, who did not have permission to play with them. When confronted, he looked from side to side as only an 11-year-old can, and seeing no escape, he admitted he had "borrowed" them and forgotten where he left them.

His forgetting was, of course, no surprise. Many of us cannot remember where our coat is five minutes after it is shed. In fact, last Monday morning at bus time when it was 20 degrees outside, after searching high and low for his coat, Jerem remembered he had forgotten that very item at his uncle's house. The problem is that my brother lives 400 miles north of us; we had been there for the weekend and weren't going back anytime soon.

I threatened to tell Denis that the binoculars were missing unless he found them within 24 hours. Yes. I fall into the shabby mother-trick of, "I'm going to tell your father." I *am* that mean, but I like to excuse myself when I'm tired, or hungry or in a hurry which is most of the time. Jerem searched everywhere. He consulted his friends with whom he plays hunting, spying and soldiering games, without luck. No one remembered. He went to bed sober and depressed that night. His last prayer before sleep was: "Dear God, please help me find those binoculars, because I *can't* remember where I left them."

That night he had a dream and relived what he was doing the last time he played with them. He saw himself in our walk-up attic where he and his friend Luke had been using them to spy on the neighbor. He had wrapped them in an old blanket to protect them and placed them behind some dusty boxes under the eaves for safe-keeping. Sensing God's presence as only a child can, he woke up that very moment knowing exactly where they were, he turned on the light and wrote himself a note as a reminder. In the morning he found the binoculars just as the dream had revealed. I never in a hundred years would have found them. He retrieved them and handing them over to me beaming and triumphant saying, "GOD ANSWERED my prayer!"

INDEED. GOD DELIVERS US in so many ways and gives us good gifts in his own perfect time. He hears the prayers and pleas of his children. There are times when I can't think why he has gifted me, a crabby, impatient mother with eternal life.

Cool Cotton Sheets

SUMMER 1997

THE OTHER DAY I stood in front of the freezer for five minutes with the door open until billows of fog began rolling out. I had forgotten what I was doing and had to shut the door, go back to the kitchen and reorient myself. Reminding myself that I needed to thaw something for supper, I went to the basement a second time. On the way I grabbed some dirty laundry to drop off, and depositing that, forgot the freezer all together. I went upstairs and stood vaguely at the sink thinking, wasn't I going to do something else down there?

It isn't only women who do this; men do the same thing. This is why you see them standing in the garage staring at the back wall for hours. They can't remember why they opened the door and walked in. Finally they give up and begin to re-shelve the tools left on the floor by the kids.

Forgetting where you are or what you're doing can be a sign of depression. The other day I went to our bedroom to water the plants and watered the trash basket instead. The next day, I took a package to UPS, paid for it and left with it under my arm. The clerk called after me; "Hey, it's okay if you really WANT to deliver that yourself, but I could probably get it there a lot faster." During times like this deciding what to wear can require as much effort as reading a software manual.

It is comforting to note that great men have often experienced the darkness of depression, and despair. Samuel Rutherford, the Puritan preacher, once wrote to a friend; "I am at a low ebb as to any sensible communion with Christ; yea, as low as any soul can be, and do scarce know where I am." In 1527 Martin Luther had nearly a year of sickness and intense depression. He was normally a prolific writer, publishing faster than most people could read. During that time his pen was silent. But out of that time came his most famous hymn, "A Mighty Fortress." He was able to find a measure of comfort in God, as one beautiful phrase reveals: "...Our helper he amid the flood of mortal ills prevailing."

As an antidote to anxiety and to find comfort during suffering Paul urges us to "Think about these things" — things that are right. Pure. Admirable. Lovely. (Phil.4:8) These "things" Paul speaks of are often found all around us — as ordinary and unremarkable as the English sparrow or a dandelion.

Jane Greer, a poet friend, notes that during a time of darkness she could see nothing good about living. In desperation she asked God to show her one thing that could make her want more of life. That noon he gave her a "thing" to think about. As she ran errands, she passed two men jogging along the street. They were older, paunchy guys with big jelly-bellies wearing nothing but Speedos and running shoes. Their little twig arms and legs were very tan, so she knew they did this often. They paused at an intersection while the light changed and did that little jig that runners do so their legs don't lock up. As they bounced there in their tight Speedos with their bellies and breasts jiggling up and down, she suddenly knew that life was worth living.

She adds, "Understand that if I were to jog (which I would NEVER do) nearly naked, these old guys would feel the same about me. God loves them and they were full of joy, as full as the most purely joyous thing I can think of, which is when my dog scratches her own back in her favorite two square feet of sweet clover with her tennis ball in her mouth, grinning."

There was a time when the psalmist wrote: "My heart is not proud, O Lord, I do not concern myself with great matters or things too wonderful for me. But I have stilled and quieted my soul; like a weaned child with its mother, like a weaned child is my soul within me" (Ps. 131:1–2).

When I am struggling to endure through some anxious and ill times, I find it is the pleasure and hope of small matters that sustain me. The everyday. The ordinary. A purple finch who sings his heart out. A perfect butter-yellow zinnia. Pure white cotton sheets dried in the sun and wind. Somehow these homey, simple things become markers in small, unexceptional packages that point to a Savior who is "altogether lovely." They remind me that a God who ministers to the tiniest bird can be trusted to care for the matters of my life and heart.

THE SUMMER HAS BEEN difficult for our family, but suffering invites us to examine foundational beliefs to see whether they are sustainable during hard times — and that is a good thing. We have not only drawn comfort from the beauty of simple things that exist in creation all around us; we are comforted by and find hope in the humanity of Jesus as he is found in the scriptures. He grew weary and thirsty, he wept with his friends when Lazarus died. Yet nothing fell through the cracks; no ship was wrecked because he couldn't make it to the disciples on time; no one missed getting healed because they had sinned too greatly or were too short to see him in the crowd.

This summer I often looked at the book of Hebrews, and especially the richness of chapter 12. We are told that you have not come to "darkness, gloom and storm; but to… Mount Zion, to the heavenly Jerusalem, the city of the living God. You have come to thousands upon thousands of angels in joyful company…" (vs 18-24). I'm not sure why the image of myriad angels singing, or doing whatever it is they do, was so powerful to me during this time. Perhaps it was the reassurance that we have been invited, too. That the brokenness and depression we suffer will not be a game-changer or a reason for us to be left outside. All this made me weep. Today, we do not feel this joy the angels have, but we hope for it. The belief that God is able to keep us, body and soul, is enough to sustain me for now.

Do Not Open
Under Pressure

AUGUST 2000

R̲ECENTLY MY HUSBAND WAS making an espresso on our machine. He actually wanted the neighborhood coffee shop to make him one, but they refused because it was 10 minutes til closing. In retrospect, perhaps he should have skipped it altogether. I could hear him in the kitchen moving around, opening cabinet doors and grinding beans.

As you probably know, a lot of steam is intentionally built up in the chamber of an espresso machine and we are expressly warned about this. In fact, there is this written in English right on the equipment: *CAUTION: Do not remove coffee filter when under pressure.* From the living room I listened to the lovely shhhhisssss followed by the intense smell of French roast wafting through the air when suddenly I heard a loud POUFF!! as if someone shot a .22 rifle into a pillow. It was followed by a faint sprinkling sound. I knew right away what happened and yelled, "ARE YOU OKAY?" I received a mournful, "Yeeesss..."

Opening the chamber before the steam has cooled causes an explosion that blows finely ground coffee all over the kitchen and anyone standing nearby. We know that now. When I arrived at the scene, Denis was on his hands and knees wiping the floor. I did not add to his misfortune by silently pointing at the warning, I just grabbed a dishcloth and began quietly wiping off the counters while keeping my face averted. I know it's not nice to enjoy another's mistake. But there was something amusing about my smart husband doing something, well, stupid.

A few days later we had another unfortunate explosion as we returned from an outing with our granddaughter in the late afternoon. Pulling the car into our garage on a bright afternoon is an act of faith. You assume everything is as you left it because the blinding light prevents you from seeing anything inside. So you aim for the darkened pit and slowly pull into the stall.

We could not see that our house painter had left a gallon of unopened white paint in the tire track. When the car hit it, there was a loud explosion, and in the micro-second that followed, Denis thought we'd blown a tire, but in the next instant white paint blasted over the front of the car and the windshield. There was paint everywhere: dripping off the tools, the tarps, the lawnmower, and the bookcase I was refinishing. The garage looked like a gigantic Jackson Pollock painting. For 30 minutes everyone worked like maniacs trying to remove the paint before it hardened.

The car is fine, but the paint permanently splashed on the garage floor will always remind us of the summer Toad Hall got painted and we ran over a can of paint. I felt badly for our house painter, but especially for Denis. He was already weary to the bone because of other difficulties, and a look of infinite tiredness came over his face, but he didn't utter one impatient word to our painter. I admired him for not even mildly cussing. The next day, he even laughed about it.

The troubles humans face are not only the life-shattering kinds; nearly everyone gets some of those. Life also gives us plenty of common, everyday trials that lead to body-and-soul weariness. In the midst of cleaning up the coffee grounds and the paint we are supposed to keep going, loving and caring for others, but eventually, the stresses of life begin to weigh too much. When I reach the margins of my coping ability, I start thinking crazy: I'm never answering the phone again. If you complain about what I've made for supper? I quit. Do not ask to visit us because I don't plan to change the sheets on the guest bed until they rot.

Even minor mishaps can make a cursing mommy out of me.

Reaching this point seems to happen every summer about the time people really need a holiday. Suddenly, I want to leave everything and run away to what J.R.R. Tolkien calls "The Last Homely House, its doors flung wide." The Last Homely House was a place of rest and refuge that existed on the edge of the dark and evil Misty Mountains through which the Hobbits had to travel. Of course, the weariness of their journey and the terrifying troubles the travelers faced made the place seem like heaven. Tolkien writes, "Bilbo would have gladly stopped there forever." Elrond's "house was perfect whether you like food, or sleep, or work, or story-telling or just sitting and thinking, or a pleasant combination of them." During their stay "their clothes were mended as well as their bruises, their tempers and their hopes."

Come Away

THE GOSPEL OF MARK tells us that on a day when Jesus' disciples were worn out from life, he tells them, (the context is instructive) "Because so many people were coming and going that they did not even have a chance to eat, he said to them, 'Come with me by yourselves to a quiet place and get some rest'" (Mark 6:31). What a beautiful invitation from the ultimate authority on weariness and the need for rest!

We recently spent a week at a lake cabin, where I could imagine settling down and staying for a long time, perhaps forever. It had all the things Tolkien mentions (except for the mending clothes part) including no visible neighbors, no telephone and no e-mail. We slept deeply without the sound of medical helicopters, sirens and buses passing our house. The planets and stars swung silently through the night as the peepers trilled and the loons called. We ate grilled chicken and fresh berries. We drank wine in the evening and read P.D. James mysteries. I sat on the dock early one morning and watched a loon preen herself just a few feet away on the water. She rolled lazily onto her back, waggled a webbed foot in the air, and probed the white feathers of her breast. How peaceful and satisfying to do nothing more than look at God's creation. For the moment, there was a quiet joy for not having any trouble of my own, and of not knowing about yours.

You Must Leave Here

HOWEVER MUCH WE WANT to stay at the Cabin, God won't allow it. Eventually we must leave again for the Misty Mountains. Throughout Scripture, God calls his people into his presence to bless and equip them for their work and calling. Then God essentially tells them: "You must go. You can't stay here. Not yet." We can imagine David as a teenager, happily (we romantically assume happy) out in the fields caring for his sheep, killing lions, writing poetry, and composing music. Then one day, out of the blue, lightning strikes this bucolic scene. The prophet Samuel calls him in and anoints him to be king over Israel. David is going to be the best king Israel ever has. His descendants will sit on the throne forever, in fact, one of them will be Jesus Christ, The Son of David, and through him all people will be blessed.

This all sounds wonderful, but think of how many treacherous mountains David had to climb after that anointing — his trouble with Saul, wars, the death of his closest friend, becoming a fugitive, feigning mental illness to save his life, political intrigue, betrayal, adultery, murder, rape, family dysfunction, and attacks on his throne by his own son. The list goes on and on.

David's honesty about life is powerful. He prays to God:

Though you have made me see troubles, many and bitter, you will restore my life again; from the depths of the earth you will again bring me up.

(Ps. 71:20)

For David to say, "You will restore my life again," implies that the things he has seen and endured (including his own sin) have taken a severe toll on his life, yet he believes God is able to to restore life again. Psalm after psalm poured out of David's heart leaving us a trail of life-saving caches to help us through the Misty Mountains. He models for us the trust in God that we desire, but often escapes us. He demonstrates that of all things, God is faithful, and he *will* bring us, not only through this life, but to life eternal.

Meanwhile, after we rest awhile, God sends us back to daily life with all of its messiness. Tolkien, in writing his great trilogy, knows how difficult it is to leave Elrond's home. How difficult to be a pilgrim. As human beings, we long for the safety and beauty of Home. It's in our bones — that memory of the first Garden. Strider, the Hobbit's guide and protector, gently corrects our impulse to stay in the cabin forever when he says of this place: "There my heart is, but it is not my fate to sit in peace, even in the fair house of Elrond." But one day — one day when the Kingdom is fully restored — we will be allowed to stay.

A Pathetic Coda

IT MAY SEEM PATHETIC that when I return to ordinary life I must repeat, week after week, a home-keeping duty I detest: grocery shopping. For a lot of reasons. It is unavoidable; we need to eat. Every week, I watch it disappear in seconds, go back and do the same thing over again and again. I run to the store, bring home bags of food, only to return immediately because I've forgotten the toilet paper, which was very plainly written on the list, and which one cannot do without because all the Puffs are gone and we've started in on the paper towels.

Another reason I dislike shopping is that certain kinds of supermarket trickery makes me angry. Recently, Hy-Vee had a type of plum which I happen to know are the best even though they are extremely ugly. They are called dinosaur eggs. The price was affordable, so I bought six. There were also some unusual peaches — little squashed round things called doughnut peaches. Again, ugly, but tasty. They were cheaper than *regular* peaches so I got a bag of them. As I was checking out and watching the totals, the plums rang up at $8.34 and the peaches were $6.80; this was *way* over my budget. At first, I was too stunned to protest. Then my eyes narrowed, and I got the feeling I was being suckered. When the checker was done, I went back to the fruit to look and sure enough the plums were *not* $1.39 a pound. They were $1.39 *Each*! The *Each* was in very small abbreviated print. Same thing with the peaches; they were $.68 *Apiece*! I felt humiliated and swindled so I just went home.

That evening I caught Denis eating one of the plums, and I shouted, "WHAT are you DOING? That plum cost a $1.39!"

He looked at it carefully and said: "Should I wait until it is rotten before I eat it?"

Later he tried to assuage my guilt for spending so much money on fruit by assuring me it was so good, he was quite sure they tasted more like $5.00 each, so actually it was a good deal.

I've always assumed that the older I got, the better I would become at most things. I thought I would balance out the need to be engaged with life and the need to find restoration and rest without capsizing first. But apparently not. I find myself obsessing over failure to read grocery store signs more carefully, and then not having the courage to return the merchandise and get my money back. Translate that kind of failure into bigger more important things like relationships and responsibilities to people and work and what it reveals is that I can be a disaster. I feel more need for wisdom and more practice in the fundamentals of love, patience and forgiveness than ever. Which is why all of the above, from Jesus' invitation to "come away" to David's confession about his troubles being many and bitter continually give me hope that with God's help, I can endure to the end.

Saint Francis de Sale's instructions apply so particularly to people like myself:

> Go on in all simplicity, do not be so anxious to win a quiet mind, and it will be all the quieter. Do not examine so closely into the progress of your soul. Do not crave so much to be perfect, but let your spiritual life be formed by your duties, and by the actions which are called forth by circumstances. Do not take overmuch thought for tomorrow. God, who has led you safely on so far, will lead you on to the end. Be altogether at rest in the loving holy confidence which you ought to have in His heavenly Providence.

Call the FBI

August 2002

A FEW YEARS AGO OUR neighbor Susan rang the doorbell — which wasn't so remarkable, but since it was the third time that day... well, the whole thing became memorable. She was looking rather worse; her hair was disheveled, her eyes had dark circles under them and she was shaking. She smelled strongly of cigarettes and mildew.

"Could I use your phone?" She sounded frightened.

I invited her inside.

"I need to call the FBI in Minneapolis," she explained on her way to the kitchen where our phone was mounted on the wall.

I knew she'd been having trouble with the neighbor on the other side of her house, and at first I thought he may have finally done something really criminal. Ted was an aggressive, angry man who harassed all of his neighbors. One time he chased our son down the street, across our yard and onto our porch because he rode his bike on newly laid asphalt in the alley. He'd almost caught up to him when Jerem slammed through the front door screaming, "DAAAAD!" The terror in his voice brought us both running. That was the kind of neighbor he was.

He particularly bullied Susan about how she kept her yard. Once, out of pure malice he aimed his paint sprayer over the fence at the freshly painted siding on her house. His paint was white. Hers was a dark pine green. When Susan found it, he loftily claimed it was wind drift and he couldn't help *that*. Susan wept because the whole back-side of her house was ruined.

It's true that Susan was a hoarder and her yard was a bit of an eyesore because she collected things other people threw away. Raccoons, squirrels, mice (and someone was sure they'd seen rats), all lived in her small yard. On the other hand, the rock wall she built along the front sidewalk and the wild cottage garden look of her flowers was a fascinating mix of chaos and beauty.

But this time, it wasn't Ted who was bothering her. She explained that someone had broken into her house and stolen all her important papers: the deed to her house, her insurance papers, the car title, bank receipts. She had searched and searched. They were nowhere to be found; she knew it had to have been a burglar. She begged us keep an eye on her home and report any suspicious activity and we promised to do it.

She had finally gone to the police station to report this theft, and they sent an officer to inspect the premises. He reported no sign of forced entry, and since there was unbroken snow in the yard surrounding the house, he could tell no one had gone in through a window. She was not reassured by this, so she went back to the station to pressure them a little more; and while she was waiting, she told me, the oddest thing happened. She left her purse on the chair for just a moment to get a drink from the fountain in the hall. When she returned she saw that someone had been rifling through her purse and had stuffed in every single missing paper back inside!

That was when she began to piece together what was going on. She knew her little house and property were very valuable being a corner lot and prime real estate. The local newspaper had reported that the Mayo Clinic was desperate for more parking space for its employees. Susan's house was only two blocks from St. Mary's, the clinic's largest hospital — so wasn't it obvious that the police and the Mayo were involved in a conspiracy to steal her property, tear down her house, and build a parking lot? However, when she was down at the station the second time, the police could see that she was not to be trifled with, and they began to have second thoughts about their methods and had found the perfect opportunity to return all her papers and then accuse *her* of being crazy.

It was so frightening to not trust the police and she so desperately needed to feel safe that she was trying to reach the FBI in Minneapolis for help and protection. When she called all she ever got was an answering machine: "Please leave your name, phone number and a brief summary of your problem and we will get back to you." Over the next several days she used our phone to call them four or five more times leaving desperate messages and begging for help. She asked us to please continue watching her house and if we saw any strangers trying to get in, to please help her. I assured her we absolutely would. Then she and I looked at each other helplessly because who do you call when you suspect a crime and the police are complicit?

She was so convincing one could almost believe her. But we knew something about Susan (who has since died from cancer): she had a mental illness. Psychiatrists had labeled her a paranoid schizophrenic. There were times when the medical model claimed that is all she was. But in getting to know her we learned she was far more than her medical diagnosis.

True, she was eccentric, and sometimes confused, but mental illness did not reflect all of who she was. We saw evidence of this again and again. She was resourceful and creative; I loved how she hauled bricks from a demolition site blocks away on an old lawnmower bed — she had replaced the engine with boards to make a platform. Trip after trip and hundreds of pounds made a huge pile in her driveway. From those bricks she laid a beautiful patio and a walk through her flowers. When her roof needed to be replaced she did it herself. Painstakingly bit by bit. Up and down the ladder, day after day, carrying a few shingles at a time. And all her neighbors shared in the disposal of her old roof because late at night as we slept she put the shingles in grocery sacks and deposited them in our trash cans. She taught me how to mix mortar and build a little garden wall with stones. She gave me a recipe for pickled crab apples. She played Jelly Roll Morton on our piano. We talked about Russian authors and argued about whether Dostoyevsky was better than Tolstoy. Many times I saw her sitting on her stone steps half-hidden behind tall ox-eye daisies and her rotting '65 Mustang ("A collector's car, you know. I've been offered thousands for it.") sorting through bags of old clothes or reading the newspaper, and I would bring her a plate of our supper to share. Her keen pleasure in the food kept me doing it again and again. To my everlasting benefit, she proved to me that even though she had a serious mental health problem, she was a beautiful human being, a good friend and God-endowed with unique gifts.

Uniquely Gifted

I THOUGHT MORE ABOUT her after watching *A Beautiful Mind,* based on the life of mathematician John Nash, because it caused me to reflect more on what it is like to have a mental illness. One of the things that struck me is how the film director almost forces the viewer to identify with the terrifying and confusing mental storms Nash endured. I remember when the camera led us out to his study, a little shack in the back yard, where we assumed Nash had been spending fruitful hours working on his research. As the door opened and we looked in, we were hopeful that we might see evidence of his recovery. Instead we saw hundreds and hundreds of bits of paper painstakingly pinned to the walls until every square inch was covered with urgent messages and codes. We knew immediately that we were seeing the terrible state of his mind. My eyes welled with tears of dread because I had grown to care about him. I saw he was more than just his illness, more than a mathematical genius: he was a man of wit and humor, a human being, who despite his suffering had extraordinary gifts in mathematics. To our wonder and delight, in real life John Nash eventually won the Nobel Prize.

I have friends who suffer from mental illnesses in varying intensities and this movie reminded me of how much they must endure in order to live, work, and relate to people, and of what courage it must take to keep on with daily life. Just as having any type chronic illness does not rule out the contributions one can make to the body of Christ, so also the one who suffers from depression, bi-polar, schizophrenia, or eating disorders has much to give that enriches our lives — the same as anyone. At the same time, as Christians, we too often contribute to their loneliness and humiliation by making it unsafe to be open about mental illnesses.

I have a friend who leans hard against recurring depression; she told me that one Sunday she walked into church and noticed a brochure on how Christians can defeat depression. Curious, she picked it up and learned the author believed that basically if you want to get well then you ought to begin by confessing your sin and bringing your life under the Lordship of Christ. Then get yourself up, dust off your hands and get on with life. Despite the risk of having to admit she struggled with depression, she talked to the pastor after the service and told him it is rarely that simple. She told him there were many reasons, other than unconfessed sin, and situations that might cause depression. One of them might be a chemical imbalance that no amount of pulling yourself together is going to fix, and that she herself was on a medication for depression and found it very discouraging to find such literature contributing to misinformation. The pastor looked at her, said nothing and moved on. That was many months ago, and the brochure still sits on the back table. Sadly, what this means for our Christian friends with mental illnesses, is that they continue to hide in our midst pretending to be okay in public while privately they suffer alone.

David Hilfiker, MD, writes that his life long experience with depression is manifested by a singular lack of joy; and yet he participates in the life of the church in prayer, worship, daily Bible reading, in corporate missions, and works as a physician to homeless men with AIDS. Some Christians insist that one of the marks of true spirituality is the joy you feel in your life. Following Christ has not done this for him. Yet he would attest that God is faithful and that it has been his Christian community who holds him dear and who represent God's love for him that keeps him going. He likens his mental illness to a spiritual paradox.

Hilfiker believes that if we can accompany one another through the messy reality of life, we understand — at certain moments of clarity — that we've been offered a profound journey of healing and wisdom. We discover that our journeys together, with all of their messiness, bring us closer to our deepest selves and to our littleness, and indeed, bring us closer to God. This is a paradox of the highest order, understood by only the deepest spiritualities: It is precisely through our brokenness that we touch God. [Source: "When Mental Illness Blocks the Spirit" www.davidhilfiker.com] I would add, that it is also through our brokenness that *God touches us.*

What I have discovered in these particular examples is more confirmation, as if it were needed, that all are made in the image of

God, and as such we have meaning and purpose beyond any objective material witness. There is a peculiar humanness which allows us to grasp at the transcendent and appreciate the beauty of creation. In turn we are able to create something even out of suffering and give it as a gift to another. Sometimes unwittingly.

The ability of the mentally ill to give gifts to others, despite their suffering, is not only observed by perceptive Christians. I was deeply moved by author Oliver Sacks, who wrote *The Man Who Mistook His Wife for a Hat*. Sacks has professed no particular faith that I am aware of, and yet he helps us see that even profoundly impaired people again and again prove to be more than just a medical case unable to transcend disease. In the midst of suffering they reveal a human soul, a hunger for the spiritual, a god-likeness for which there is no satisfactory scientific explanation.

As a clinical neurologist, Dr. Sacks recounts with compassion and insight the lives of people who have suffered incredible adversity — patients whose lives seem to have no meaning but suffering from neurological illness. He tells about a man whose experience of amnesia was so profound, he had no "day before." Jimmy's face expressed infinite sadness and loss, but when asked how he felt, could not tell whether he "felt badly or not." He had lost all ability to organize or remember the present. He could not remember isolated items more than a few minutes.

One day Sacks asked the sisters at the Catholic Home where Jimmy lived whether they thought he had a soul. They were outraged by the question and said he should watch Jimmy in chapel and then judge for himself. He wrote of this:

"I was profoundly moved and impressed because I saw here an intensity and steadiness of attention and concentration that I had never seen before in him or conceived him capable of. I watched him kneel and take the Sacrament on his tongue, and could not doubt the fullness and totality of Communion, the perfect alignment of his spirit with the spirit of the Mass. Fully, intensely, quietly, in the quietude of absolute concentration and attention, he entered and partook of the Holy communion. He was no longer at the mercy of… meaningless memory traces — but was absorbed in an act, an act of his whole being, which carried feeling and meaning in an organic continuity and unity, a continuity and unity so seamless it could not permit any break."

And always for a while after communion his mood of quietness and peace would persist in a way not seen in the rest of his life at the Home.*

Uniquely Fallen

IN THE CHURCH WE often avoid those who suffer from mental illnesses — the very ones who often already suffer as outcasts from family, friends, and community. They are even cast aside by their own souls; yet our privilege is to call them beloved of Christ and integral to our body. It isn't only that they need us, we need *them* if we are to believe Scripture. Paul writes, 'Those parts of the body which seem weaker are indispensable' (I Cor 12:22).

It would be misleading if I didn't make a confession. I have discovered a contemptible prejudice in myself. It may be similar to a racial bigotry you think you don't have until a particular moment reveals what is really in your sorry little heart. An example would be driving I-94 between Minneapolis and Madison, WI, when a new Cadillac with Illinois vanity plates saying *Mopeas* blows past, do I think: Retired Fat Guy from Chicago? No. I think Drug Dealer from the North Side.

---

* For further reading, note an interview with Oliver Sacks, (also author of *Awakenings* which was made into a movie starring Robin Williams) "The Fully Immersive Mind of Oliver Sacks," *Wired Magazine* April, 2002.

My prejudice against mental illness began as a revelation at the doctor's office when I was referred to a psychiatrist to renew a sleep medication that is often prescribed for people who have fibromyalgia. (One of the symptoms is sleep disorder.) At first I thought, "no problem." Whatever it takes. Then I went home and began to fuss. A psychiatrist! What did she *really* have in mind? She was looking at me funny. On the surface it was a meds consult, but was that her true agenda or does she think I'm crazy?

My appointment made me really nervous. I sat in the doctor's office trying to sit still. I told myself to stop swallowing my spit and keep my hands off my face, but I couldn't. The psychiatrist was a young man, almost too young to be my son. I wondered what he was doing there, he looked like a model from Abercrombie & Fitch. He kept his handsome face carefully neutral, as he leaned forward a bit and spoke from behind his big desk, "I will be taking notes as we talk and I don't want you to worry about that." Well....until you *mentioned* it. He paused to stare intently at me until I wondered if there was something stuck in my teeth. Then he said, "So. Why do you think you're here today?" Feeling insulted and irrational I nearly said: "Because I started my husband's bed on fire?" Regaining control in the nick of time, I carefully reported: "My doctor said it was to consult with you about this medication and also to see whether you think I should be referred to bio-feedback for muscle relaxation therapy. If she had other reasons she didn't mention them." (Maybe just a tiny bit hostile.)

My mind was racing ahead wondering how many invasive questions he would ask and whether it was safe to be honest. Does he think I am a crazy 50-something woman with a hysterical, hypochondrical personality? Oh. Isn't that a symptom of paranoia? But what if I am? Wouldn't it be safe to face it there? Should I be ashamed to get help if I needed it?

He did ask me about depression and other moods. I decided to be honest and admitted that "Anxiety is my chiefest, most nuts, biggest physical/spiritual/mental flaw." I plunged on, "Or character defect. Whatever you'd like to call it. I work hard at not being anxious and this here is making me damn nervous." He nodded and scribbled away. Now to his credit and none to mine, he was kind, insightful and he also cleverly sniffed out my evasions. After about 20 minutes I had stopped sweating and gulping air. By the end of the hour he okayed the meds and told me with a grin that I didn't need to see him again. I still left feeling like I'd been rescued from Desolation Island in the Antarctic Ocean. Just to breath air in the parking lot was exhilarating.

The more I reflected on my reaction to this insignificant encounter, the more I realized how revealing my attitude was. It is just fine for you to have any number of mental illnesses. As our four year-old granddaughter says, "I am your fren." From bi-polar to simple depression, I am okay with you having it. It doesn't make you less of a person. Blah, blah, blah. And then I had that little trick played on me, and found out it isn't okay for me, and suddenly I have to confess how sorry I am to be this kind of bigot.

And now that I think of it, the courage of some of my friends who have had to be hospitalized, therapied, medicated, sent to group with clueless "facilitators" and know-nothing "peers" is surpassing wonderful bravery. And I thank them for understanding my fear better than anyone and for continuing to be my friend despite my prejudices. In turn, I promise that I will *never* say again, when expressing relief about some medical diagnosis, "I'm so glad it wasn't in my *head!*"

Finally, one last plug. There is a book... are you surprised? *Resurrecting the Person: Friendship and the Care of People with Mental Health Problems* by John Swinton. Called a book of practical theology, Swinton issues a challenge to the church to think and act differently toward people and families whose lives have been radically altered by their encounters with mental health problems. He explores ways of separating people from their pathologies both practically and conceptually. He suggests Jesus as a model for countercultural friendship with those who have been marginalized and alienated by society.

Although I do not agree entirely with his theology, I can't find anything on the market so personally helpful and hopeful when it comes to exploring deep and meaningful friendship with a person who struggles with a mental health problem. I strongly recommend this book for anyone. We should be starving for this kind of help. We need it for the sake of Jesus. For the sake of his bride, the church. Who knows when you yourself may suffer from an unwanted mental illness?

Skirting the Fleece
WINTER 2011

"COME NOW, LET US reason together… though your sins are like scarlet, they shall be as white as snow; though they are red as crimson, they shall be like wool" (Isa. 1:18). When I was a kid I must have sung the chorus set to this verse about a million times. The perfect prescription for making the words sound like a robot on Zoloft. Not that I'm more holy because they don't sound that way to me.

I love these words because they tell us some interesting things about God. In the first phrase, he invites us to consider a pretty uncomfortable topic. God says, "let's talk about your conduct, Margie: your life and matters." Take any standard of morality — even the low bar you set up yourself, and let's say nothing about the Ten Commandments, and then tell me how that's working for you. Can you have this conversation or are you afraid I can't take care of what you've done and love you at the same time? Give me your best shot.

God's desire to communicate on such a personal level is staggering. The invitation is radiant. It deconstructs my prickly defense and causes me to listen.

"WHITE AS SNOW," I understand. We have a lot of it right now; you probably do, too. All I need to do is look out the window. But to sharpen the analogy, in case we don't understand snow, God mentions wool for us to consider. "...Though your sins are red as crimson, they shall be like wool." Did you know crimson and scarlet are color-fast dyes? You can't change your mind once they get into a fiber. They are indelible. When wool is first sheared from a sheep it is not a brilliant shade of white or even cream, so I needed help enriching this analogy.

If we lived in an agrarian culture and raised sheep we might understand it better. We might know what skirting a fleece means. I didn't until two years ago, when Anita became our housemate, friend and Ransom's resident assistant.

Some of the delight of having her around is that you never know what is next — like right now in Mole's End, her living quarters, there are 27 ugly, creepy worms gorging on mulberry leaf mash. These waxy creatures each have a small dark cord pulsing down the center of their backs; more creepy. They are silk worms, about to spin the cocoons that make one of the earth's most exquisite fibers.

So anyway, last spring when she hauled in several giant gunny sacks of sheep fleece purchased from some flock owner and began prepping them for spinning by dumping them onto a large tarp in the back yard, I wondered how she'd ever get wool mittens and sweaters out of that filth. The first thing she had to do was to skirt the fleece.

Raw fleece stinks and is filthy with bits of straw and dung stuck to it here and there. The color is often an unpleasant shade of stained yellow. Skirting, the first step in cleaning, is to remove the organic matter and snip away the worst of the stains. I had no idea this work was part of what makes that creamy-white sheepskin tossed on the seat of my rocking chair so attractive and comfortable on a cold day.

It was after Anita skirted, then washed all the filth out of the fleece, rinsed it, and put it out to dry in the sun that the transformation became so apparent. [You can watch Anita do this on youtube: "Cleaning Wool Fleece" www.youtube.com/watch?v=dOW9bW-BAlIY] It's beauty shone. It smelled natural and fresh and the color was almost pure white.

So right out of the shepherd culture where Isaiah lived, God chose to link the forgiveness of our sins, all our wrong-doing — even as recent as last night when I unnecessarily commented on a woman passing our table in a café, calling her a thoroughly nasty, descriptive name — to a process everyone understood. This transformation is part of what God means when He says your sins "shall be as wool."

Come Away with Me

BEING MARRIED TO ONE person for 43 years is a part of my life's story. Wouldn't you think that after so long Denis and I wouldn't have much skirting to do? That we'd pretty much be white as wool?

Here is a little of how it works for us, and how sometimes it doesn't...

Last November — on vacation. The quietness and beauty of the North Shore invites heart repair, renewal and re-creation.

First day. I did nothing, unless absolutely necessary. Like going to the bathroom. Didn't make the bed or wash a single dish. Denis did that. We read. Stared out the window at the rocky shore and the sky. Went for a walk. Saw a big buck lying in the woods just outside the door, his antlers were framed by bracken and tall grass. A bald eagle flew past the window. I didn't cook. Supper menu: half a smoked whitefish; rice crackers; carrot sticks. There was no hurry in anything we did.

Second through fourth day. Although we're on vacation we need to do marriage care. Busyness, distance, offensive tones of voice, thoughtless reactions have built up. Like skirting a fleece, Denis and I must pick off the weeds stuck to our skin, the pieces of shit, the yellowed bits of marriage in need of washing. Sorry if you thought otherwise. Reconnecting in love and attachment isn't like eating vanilla pudding — a swish of the tongue and wow you've eaten a quart; sometimes it takes all we have to remain attached and in love. It's work we don't really want to do when we'd rather be getting on with the fun stuff of vacation. On the other hand, 43 years have taught us that it must be part of life and we're grateful that being where we are makes it possible to sit down opposite one another with a glass of wine, pen and paper, the book we're reading, and talk. God is in the midst of us with his invitation and promise, though sometimes I forget that.

A THERAPIST FRIEND RECOMMENDED a book: *Hold Me Tight* by Sue Johnson. (I like to think the title is the fault of the publisher's marketing department.) Johnson, a clinical psychologist, developed something called Emotionally Focused Couple Therapy (EFCT). It has a simple message: Forget about learning how to argue better, analyze your early childhood, make grand romantic gestures, or experiment with new sexual positions. Instead, get to the emotional underpinnings of your relationship by recognizing that you are emotionally attached to and dependent on your partner in much the same way a child is on a parent for nurturing, soothing, and protection. In this book she teaches EFCT through a series of conversations and practical exercises to help couples create more secure and lasting bonds.

I'm pleased that her ideas helped us find ways to express what was troubling us and move us a little closer toward understanding and change. All of us hunger for safe emotional connections; we are hard bit with this need like it's in our blood, our DNA; it's part of the inescapable image of God implanted within us. We long for it even more than food or sex. (Don't argue with me about that.) In marriage, Johnson writes, "Distressed partners may use different words but they are always asking the same basic questions: 'Are you there for me? Do I matter to you? Will you come when I need you, when I call?'"

These questions are almost exactly the ones Denis and I have used to describe this generation's hunger for love and commitment in relationships. We've observed that the answer to these questions in so many instances is silence or abandonment by parents, lovers, friends, employers. In other words, no one will be there for you. I instantly recognize myself; it describes what I want from marriage. Denis does, too. We both want the answer to be: "Always."

As DENIS AND I read the book together, listened (that's *hard* work) to one another, and examined what the author calls "Demon Dialogues," we saw our own ways of going round and round a raw spot, arguing about exactly who said or did what. We want the other person to acknowledge our point and agree, but it ends up looking like the only way out is to admit you're the rotten spouse every single time. We end up me angry and hostile, him withdrawn and cold. I know what that's called: fight or flight. We're not proud of it.

We couldn't have scripted the spontaneous exchange of one afternoon. Even as it happened, we knew it was a stupid-funny thing to quibble about. But it captured the essence of deeper struggles:

D: What time is it?

M: (I pick up my cell and look at the analog clock on the front.) 5:30. Er, no. 6:30? Hmmm. (I look again because the hands are close.)

D: (Whips out his cell showing the time in digits.) 5:34. *This* is better.

(The instant he said that I knew a look of hostility crossed my face. He saw it. In that second we understood where this was going and we chose to keep talking, and laughing at the absurdity of it.)

M: You've made a value judgment: your way is "better." Therefore, my choice of analog is: *Not* "better." Mine is *Less* better. It's not the *right* way. I'm wrong, therefore, I'm stupid — in your mind. But I'M NOT STUPID.

D: No! That's not what I meant. It has *nothing* to do with value judgment. There may be a ton of reasons why you'd have the other. In fact, one might be that it's more aesthetically pleasing. So saying "This is better" wasn't meant to be a personal dismissal or condemnation of what you've chosen.

M: But c'mon, when you say something is *better*, what do you mean by using that word? I have lots of trouble getting away from the feeling that I've just been, yeah, in a small way, but, still, I've been judged. Words *mean* something.

D: It's not like that at all. In fact... (I notice how he says " in fact" but talks about emotion. It's kinda endearing.) ...it hurts me that you immediately assume the worst. It's fine to have something different, I only meant that when you glance at it, digital is easier to read.

We recognize that Denis likes clarity and preciseness more than I do. Control is important, too, because maybe if one can be very careful about details, why then one can stay the heck out of personal catastrophes. He's hurt because he wants me to trust that he *doesn't* think I'm stupid. I'm hurt because he said, "This is better." If I can be "right" about things, then it proves I've made a good choice and maybe he will love me more. Being a people-pleaser means if I can just figure out how to keep the laws around here, why then everybody's gonna be really happy and really love me. Oy vey.

Both of us gain insight that can help our relationship. I've got to calm down and not so quickly assume he's purposely being an, an, well, insensitive. He needs to use better word choice. But beneath it all we need to remember what we both want is to be the other's love above all others.

Annoying You

THERE ARE TIMES IN the midst of a conflict when I feel like running away, but even in this, God understands why the human heart sometimes wants to escape. On what must have been a bad day the psalmist writes: "Oh that I had the wings of a dove! I would fly away and be at rest" (Ps. 55:6).

Often, on the morning after a difficult day, I read signs of the Holy Spirit's presence with us. I'm definitely calmer. I know we'll never be perfect, but we're mending, and I see my spouse with refreshed eyes. The habits that annoyed yesterday are strangely tolerable again, maybe even a little charming. Thankfully, my own sins are "as wool," they've been forgiven. I send Denis a quote from a comedian: "I love being married. It's so great to find that one special person you want to annoy for the rest of your life."

A friend muses how funny-odd that sometimes seeing your spouse through another's eyes causes renewed appreciation. We watch them kindly pick up a child and offer a drink, or hear them patiently explain how to recover a lost file, or deliver a really fine lecture and we are touched that the person speaking is our friend and lover.

I KNOW A BOOK is not going to be the answer to every problem nor is Johnson's EFCT, though it has been helpful. Through the years Denis and I have reasoned with one another and with God in search of a place of beauty for our love and commitment. We long to be bright and beautiful wool ready to be spun into all manner of artful coverings in service to one another and to Christ.

Part of this service to one another, and to you, is truth-telling. Years of Christian practice, being in a ministry — neither guarantees a clean easy marriage. Rather, here in the midst of dust and wounds, we meet Christ and find life and hope in his promise to make all things new again.

Consider This

ADVENT 1994

*E*IGHT HUNDRED YEARS BEFORE Christ was born, Isaiah prophesied that out of the tribe of Judah, from Jesse, the father of King David, would come a shoot. A descendant. He would be a root growing out of dry ground. In a landscape of death the "Rose of Sharon" would grow. It would be so splendid and so deeply rooted it would redeem men from their darkness and rescue creation from the fall. Its might would extend not only to the great griefs and tragedies of all time, but to the everyday illnesses and trials of our lives. We are still waiting for the consummation of this regeneration plan begun before the foundation of time and revealed in Bethlehem 2,000 years ago.

Consider Poison Ivy

A BEAUTIFUL, WAXY-GREEN PLANT with dark leaves arranged in patterns of three. Without care or fertilizer, it can form a dense ground cover, stand as a single healthy plant or even become a deeply rooted vine twisting up a tree. It produces attractive clusters of creamy white berries. In fall, it turns a tempting red. It could look lovely in an arrangement or even a garden except for its toxic oils and the havoc it wrecks on human skin.

Why did God make it?

No one wonders more than our son, Jerem, who regularly experiences this form of broken creation, if it is that. He rides a mountain bike with friends whenever he can — 180 mph straight down the Mississippi River bluffs resplendent with poison ivy. It is inevitable that while hurtling down the slopes he will wipe out in a luxurious patch. From these accidents he will contract a raving case of itching blisters every time. After his most recent wipeout, I heard a lot of scratching and complaining, until his uncle recommended a cure which Jerem followed to the letter.

A day or so later, a friend, a young doctor-friend, noticed the bright, red weeping condition of his legs and asked what happened. It looked like third-degree burns.

Jerem replied he was curing himself of poison ivy: You should know this, he said, in case you get a patient with poison ivy. You take a *3-M* pot scrubber, soak it in *Undiluted* bleach, and use it to *Scratch* until the blisters come *Right Off!* The poison ivy is *Gone!* (And voila! You have replaced it with third-degree burns instead? Thanks, Uncle Dallas. Do not try this at home.)

Our young doctor-friend frowns on home remedies and suggested a simple application of steroid cream might be more effective in countering the effects of the fall.

Consider a Tooth

CONSIDER SOMETHING SO SMALL as a tooth: a bit of hard enamel surrounded by sensitive pulp seated in bone and used for grinding and tearing. Despite its size, there is nothing like the pain of a tooth to get your attention during the night hours, when you cry out to God and promise to leave off all your addictions if only he will stop your suffering. When it finally gets so bad you can no longer stand it, you call a dentist, and you can be sure you will need to pay her hundreds of dollars to also pay attention to it.

My trouble was a broken molar. It started last June and to this day it still hurts. I wonder why we just didn't pull it out and be done with it. (Another home remedy?)

In August I finally got it capped with gold. Why gold? Because, "It might need a root canal and gold is easier to drill through." Okay.

When I returned for the final fitting the dentist patiently tried to seat this new cap in the back of my mouth which was benumbed, wide-open, sheathed in plastic skirting, and bedecked with numerous sucking, spraying and drilling instruments which hung off my lips. With each try his gloves grew slipperier until he dropped the cap in the back of my throat. I was so alarmed, thinking I was going to inhale the thing and die right there, I half sat up and coughed hard. (My last name is not Haack for nothing.) The gold cap shot across the room where it hit the wall and skidded under a table.

We were all embarrassed. My dentist apologized profusely, cleaned it off, reached in my mouth and dropped it again. That time I was ready for him and simply closed my throat and stopped breathing.

Unbelievably, he did it a third time. He felt bad, but not enough to give me his services for free.

I went home to wait and things got worse. When I went back, sure enough, I needed to see an Endodontist for a root canal. (I didn't know people were making a special living just by sucking out tooth nerves.) Suffice it to say that a small piece of enamel and dentine can create more pain than one thought possible, ruin a vacation, and be an excellent reminder that I need deliverance from this body just to be rid of my teeth.

Consider Relationships

AND LEST YOU THINK I am so silly as to believe redemption is only about weeds and broken teeth — consider relationships. How their sadness and grief often causes us to cry! Recently, Jerem, who is now a senior in high school and feeling the conflict between his growing independence and parental authority, left the house one day in a black funk. When he returned, he had a surprising and unusual request for us. He had run into a friend who'd been homeless for two weeks. (Reasons are private except to say that there's been grief in his family's life.) Jerem wondered if we would consider letting him live with us. It was startling because we were under the impression that no one would *want* to live with us — *if* they had a choice.

Despite already having two adolescents, which is more than enough any time, we agreed to a trial period and possibly more. Perhaps God is drawing this young man to himself. Perhaps his way to regeneration lies through our living room and pantry. We pray so.

Consider Carson

FINALLY, CONSIDER A BABY. My youngest nephew, Carson is a child to melt any woman's heart. At just over a year he looks innocent enough to eat butter and never have it melt in his mouth.

Carson has a peculiar trait — at least it is peculiar to me since I am a woman. He doesn't *like* women. Oh, he likes his mother well enough and he tolerates his sisters, but all other females are completely scorned. Since he will have nothing to do with us, we aunts have perversely enjoyed teasing him. He adores his daddy and is very pleasant with men and boys. There seems no reason for this other than it is just Carson being Carson.

One Sunday as I sat beside him during church, he quietly squirmed around on his father's lap and noticed I was sitting too close. My arms were crossed and I was concentrating on prayer when he scowled and slapped my hand. Startled, I looked up. His grinning father leaned over to me and whispered, "He needs to get saved."

Stifling my laughter, I thought of how much what Carson's father said was true. After all, even cute little Carson will need to be rescued from himself, like any of us. As babies we are neither innocent nor perfect. Yet, many parents are shocked to find they have actually passed their broken natures on to their children even as the Bible says we will. David laments, I was "sinful at birth, sinful from the time my mother conceived me." (Ps. 52:5) We don't just grow into sin. It is in us from the beginning. Intrinsic. Genetic. Innate.

Consider A Flower

SOME OF MY EARLIEST memories from childhood are of things I purposely did that I knew were wrong. I am still ashamed of them and try not to think too much about them. I believe by faith they truly are put away "as far as the east is from the west," like God says. But one day I am really going to *know* it.

When I remember them and all the ones that have accumulated up to this day, I think of Jesus, that root of Jesse. "A shoot will come up from the stump of Jesse, from his roots a Branch will bear fruit" (Isa. 11:1).

I have grown to love that shoot — that flower sprung out of dry ground. Some day I shall be whole, because he has redeemed me. I am fruit. Small, maybe, but fruit nevertheless.

Although consummation is not yet complete, I see it coming. And with it "creation itself will be liberated from its bondage to decay and brought into the glorious freedom of the children of God" (Rom.8:21).

Poison Ivy effects — healed.

Toothaches — healed.

Broken families — healed.

Sins — bleached away like freshly laundered sheets on the line. When the Infant Jesus returns as Christ the Lord, he will be "dispelling with glorious splendor the darkness ev'ry where."

This ancient carol by an anonymous German composer sings that beautiful message of Christmas — ever new, ever healing:

Lo, how a Rose e'er blooming
From tender stem hath sprung!
Of Jesse's lineage coming
as men of old have sung.
It came, a flowret bright,
Amid the cold of winter,
When half-spent was the night.
Isaiah 'twas foretold it,
The Rose I have in mind;
With Mary we behold it,
The virgin mother kind.
To show God's love a right
She bore to men a Savior,
When half-spent was the night.
This flow'r, whose fragrance tender
with sweetness fills the air,
Dispels with glorious splendor
the darkness ev'ry where.
True man, yet very God,
From sin and death he saves us
And lightens ev'ry load.

(From *CAROLS*, IVP, 1978)

Down the Rabbit Hole

SUMMER 2005

"**A**RE YOU FROM THE Unitarian Church?"

A small, dark-haired woman drinking a soy latte and holding a copy of *Enlightenment* magazine smiled encouragingly at me. Others seated around the table at Dunn Bros Coffee shop stared at me and waited.

I'd only been there 30 seconds before I discerned this would *not* be a discussion I controlled. I'd never been mistaken for a Unitarian. Did I look like a Unitarian? I wasn't wearing a batik jersey dress with Kokopelli on the front.

The evening before I'd seen the movie *What The Bleep Do We Know?!* with our small group from church. It was a part of a local film festival. Although it doesn't work artistically, it brings up all the big questions about life and meaning. It asks them in your face and then gives you a set of postmodern answers. We stayed up late wondering how many of our neighbors and colleagues believed or acted on these ideas — and if they did, how we could engage them in conversation and communicate Christian beliefs to them.

Before we parted, someone mentioned that the next afternoon at Dunn Bros Coffee there was a public discussion on *What the Bleep* being sponsored by the film group. I decided to join them. Life can be way too sheltered in our climate-controlled Christian community; I needed a shot of live, uncensored non-Christians talking about life and ideas. It could be a Saint Paulish Mars Hill spy-trip. I would listen, learn, and at the right moment, I could give a gorgeous presentation of the gospel.

Think Stephen Hawking on an Acid Trip

WHAT THE BLEEP Do We Know?! is a movie about quantum mechanics, sort of. My brain contains a file titled Quantum Mechanics, but it's empty — except for a scrap of corrupted information about atoms unexpectedly leaving their assigned places, or a particular atom being in several places at once. (This is a feature every parent would like, but is, apparently, possessed only by children and atoms.) So, scientists tell us, if you deliberately focus on an atom and try to catch her doing this trick she is standing still. And that is, like, just a tiny piece of a fascinating science with links to time, reality, origins, spirituality, and... truly, what the bleep do I know?

The movie is part documentary, part story, and part animation. Amanda, played by Marlee Matlin, finds herself in a weird, *Alice in Wonderland*-like experience when her daily, uninspired life literally begins to unravel, revealing the uncertain world of the quantum field hidden behind her normal, waking reality. Fourteen scientists and mystics are interviewed throughout the film and their ideas are woven together to emphasize the film's underlying concept of the interconnectedness of all things. They serve as a type of Greek chorus and introduce the Big Questions of Life as the story leads us down the "rabbit hole." Several of the experts mention there appears to be a "Silent Observer" behind the energies of the universe, but most agree they don't know for certain what makes the universe run. At the conclusion, one of the experts, known as Ramtha, looks into the camera and tells us there is no way for humans to determine what is right or wrong, and that believing in a God who will judge or punish a person for what they have done is ridiculous, because everyone chooses their own path, their own reality. That, she says, is the beginning of wisdom.

CRITICS DIFFERED WIDELY ON the film's success. Peter Howell of the Toronto Star wrote, "The film with the year's most unfortunate title also happens to be a candidate for the worst film of the year." Critic Susan Granger said, "Provocative movies like this open a world of knowledge and ideas, stimulating thinking and conversation."

What I didn't know that Sunday afternoon when I joined the film discussion was that this independent movie is the work of students of the channeler, J.Z. Knight, who calls herself Ramtha. Ramtha is a 35,000 year-old wise man, who appeared in Knight's kitchen on an afternoon in 1977. She's been channeling him ever since. Of the 14 interviewees, a number either work for or teach in her School of Enlightenment. Others who don't work for her organization, as in the case of David Albert, professor and director of the Philosophical Foundations of Physics program at Columbia University, claim they were completely misrepresented in the movie. "It became clear to me they believe that... by positive thinking we can alter the structure of the world around us. I spent a long time explaining why that isn't true, going into great detail. But in the movie, my views are turned around 180 degrees."

FOR THAT AFTERNOON DISCUSSION, I hadn't yet done this research. But even if I knew all there was to know about quantum physics and

Transcendental Meditation there's a limit to my capacity. However, my intellectual limitations aren't an excuse for never engaging with non-Christians unless it's in a controlled environment like a Bible study where there's no risk for me. It's more of a challenge to believe God is with me in a coffee shop when I'm missing my PhD, my research, and a brilliant mind.

I take heart from Jonathan, King Saul's son. When he was scouting a high-tech Philistine military out-post, he was out-gunned, out-manned, and in a suicidal position to attack. But he said to his attaché, basically, "With God, the odds on winning don't matter, so why don't we do a little rock-climbing and see what happens?" I love his armor-bearer's response: "I'm with you heart and soul!" No military strategist would have predicted the resulting disaster for the Philistines. That's reality in every dimension, including quantum mechanics: God controls the universe. He's also pleased to use people who aren't power brokers in any way — which means I'm a player. The gospel's power to save doesn't depend on my comprehension of physics or neopaganism. I can show up with my heart and soul even when it's a risky, blundering piece of rock-climbing.

Define God

THERE WERE NINE OF US — I was the lone stranger among them. (It was instructive to think about how a visitor to a Bible study might feel.) The only person I knew was a friend who quietly slipped in beside me about halfway through the discussion. She observed everything, so I can't pretend to be the next Francis Schaeffer for the sake of looking good.

I wanted to remain anonymous, listen quietly, and scope out how hostile they'd be if they knew I was a Christian. I was barely seated with an Americano when, together, they focused on me: "When did you see the movie? How did you hear about it? How many times have you seen it? What did you think? Did you like it?"

I tried to evade answering with a modest: "I really want to hear what you guys think of the movie" — they totally ignored that, like they knew I was stalling. They insisted on knowing who I was. I told them, "I saw the movie the first time last night with a group of friends from our church." (nervously adding) "We regularly get together to discuss movies, popular culture, and other things" (other things being the BIBLE which I didn't say). That prompted another chorus of questions: "What did they think about it? Did they like it? Hey, are you from the Unitarian Church?"

The last question was delivered with such anticipation and pre-approval, I felt a little ashamed dashing their hopes. I took a long noisy sip of coffee. No one had ever confused me with a Unitarian. I've noticed that evangelicals generally despise Unitarians: "Why BOTHER?" they say. "Just join the country club or the music guild, but don't PRETEND to be religious." At the same time I wondered; are we so isolated and insular that it's preposterous for me to be a Christian and yet someone who takes questions of art and culture seriously?

Finally, I replied: "No. I'm a Presbyterian. Not from the big church, the little one over on 14th street… we thought the ideas in the movie were fascinating and talked for hours about how you know that you know, how to define reality, and how to describe the soul."

They looked extremely pleased with me, like I'd just given them deep muscle massage for free. I was among pagans, but I could see they were interesting and smart. So with the next breath, I prudently admitted I hadn't the slightest capacity for discussing molecular biology, quantum physics, hormone receptors, or any other philosophical explanations for the nature of existence.

Everyone assured me they weren't "experts" either, then talked about how much they loved the movie. And how at first the main character, Amanda, was afraid of the interconnected reality that existed on an atomic level. Was reality just the reaction of her hormones on her cell receptors? Was it some other mysterious energy that lay beyond her senses? Amanda was hoping to find answers before she cracked up. One of her most painful questions was why her husband was so unfaithful — beginning from the very day of their wedding. The film group thought his infidelity was the result of Amanda's choices whether she recognized it or not. It was merely the path she had to travel to finally reach peace.

I choked a little and wondered if I needed to assert, "This makes no sense. Her husband was a jerk, he hurt her deeply because — label it whatever you want — we are moral creatures who instinctively recognize betrayal and injustice. There are absolutes. This is one of them: a groom doesn't ever, EVER get to screw around on his wedding day. Or any other time, okay? So why are you making HER responsible for this pain?" Instead, I made myself very quiet, and so I wouldn't roll my eyes. I stared down my nose into my coffee mug.

A thin man with an unruly mop of long, gray hair, his shoulder in a sling seemed to sense my conflict, looked at me with rheumy eyes; he offered this solution, "The only time I experience happiness and freedom from pain is when I meditate. I get into that zone where there is nothing. Where the mind is just blank. I do this every day." He looked so sweet. There were nods of sympathy around the table.

The cheerful woman, the one holding *Enlightenment* magazine, (later she showed us advertisements for the movie with conferences based on it being held across the country) said, "You see?! He (the thin man) is creating his own reality! He has options! We all have choices that enable us to choose our paths in spite of pain or what others do to us. To do that you go 'inner' — inside yourself — where you find your own gods."

At this point, some Christians would loudly declare Jesus Christ is LORD. Although that is my belief with every molecule of my heart, a microsecond's reflection told me that wouldn't convert them. In fact, they probably wouldn't see the point. I would only succeed in alienating them.

Instead, I summoned courage and asked, "I'd like to understand what you mean by 'gods.' I think of God as a being outside myself."

A lady in a purple sweater and a white dandelion head told me, "Well, god is *you*. It's your peptides and hormones. It's a power inside you that causes you to do certain things."

From the movie I remembered a bizarre animation of hormones pouring out of a large man's body, which made him stand over a table at a wedding reception uncontrollably stuffing food into his mouth until it dribbled down his front and bloated his belly. The idea that, on the one hand, we can't help being controlled by hormones and yet have power to stop them when they tempt us to do things which aren't socially acceptable, seemed to arbitrarily place more value on certain behaviors when, in fact, there shouldn't be a problem with whatever one's hormones choose. Or with whatever happens. Which seemed inconsistent, but they didn't notice. It made me a little crazy.

The lady in purple continued, "You have the power to control your response on the receptors of each and every one of your cells. We *have* options. We can choose our own path and we become whatever god we want to be."

It was a good thing I didn't think of a cynical response until the next day — I'd like to be god of passwords so I never have to tell some geek I forgot mine, and then be asked to tell the secret answer to my secret question which I also forgot. Debbie, a young social worker at the end of table, said, "I liked the scientists, especially the one in front of the fireplace who explained that the brain doesn't necessarily recognize reality. For the brain to see something, like, say, a clipper ship on the sea... well, it can't see a clipper ship on the sea if it's never seen one before, can it? What we see, what we know, is conditioned by culture and experience, so if we've never seen a ship before and let's say we're a Native American standing on the beach and Columbus is pulling into port, the ship doesn't exist for the brain."

I felt sad not to offer a more compelling argument, "But if you can't see the ship because the brain has no categories for it, then how can we even conceive the question humans ask all the time — What IS that? Do you think this means that reality can't exist outside our own ability to perceive it? And if reality is only imagined, how would we explain the viruses brought by Columbus, which killed so many Native Americans? Were they real or not?"

A man in flannel shirt and blue jeans had a point, "I'm a hunter." (He was allowed to admit that in this group? I was intrigued.) "And, once, years ago I took a friend into the woods. He'd never been hunting before. He couldn't see anything. Couldn't see game at all even though it was right in front of us! Only when I helped him, pointed to a deer, could he see it. His brain couldn't see because, well, he hadn't the experience. His eyes saw, but didn't REALLY see because he had no categories in which to place it."

Someone responded, "And we can't judge what's right or what's wrong for another person. It's personal choice."

This seemed so random, I changed the subject. "So, who is the Silent Observer they talk about in the movie?"

Debbie answered: "The Silent Observer is what I call my soul. I'm not good at listening to it. My soul observes what I know and wants me to take a chance on what I don't know, a chance for a better path. But I don't make that choice because I'm comfortable with the misery I already know. And life has been pretty miserable lately." (She began to cry, and the person next to her put a hand on her arm.) "Although it's only in a small way there's a natural goodness in my soul, deep down — something all people have. In that goodness, I move toward healing and try to help others become aware of that goodness in them so they can be healed. In this way I have hope that the world too, will be healed."

Moving Tectonic Plates

HERE WERE PEOPLE SINCERELY trying to make sense of a world of suffering, trying so hard to do what was right. Would they suddenly see the freedom hidden in the gospel's verdict if I told them, "All have sinned and fallen short of the glory of God"? Would they understand that if, indeed, our path to salvation depends on our ability to think positively, meditate, control hormone receptors, listen to the soul (which you can never perfectly do) — then aren't we merely committing ourselves to a new law, a works-righteousness system which can never be kept? And that what we all need is a cosmic, divine, mysterious rescue from a perfect and powerful source outside ourselves? No, they wouldn't understand. But you need to start somewhere. I relate to honesty and humility, perhaps they would, too.

I finally said, "I admire your virtue, Debbie, but to be honest? I'm ashamed because, my natural inclinations don't move toward the Good at all. If the practice of Goodness is left to me, I'm ruined, and so is the world. Take the smallest, most insignificant thing — I'm naturally selfish and I channel..." (probably the wrong word to use in that group) "...anger, hate, impatience. I don't think peptides and hormones entirely explain this inner motion toward evil. Just the other night I was so completely, disproportionately angry because this friend took the wrong way to our destination. It took all my power not to yell and grab the steering wheel. I vowed never to be in a car with this person again unless I was driving — all because it made us two minutes late. So if we depend on *me* to improve humanity even the slightest, we're doomed. God, help me." And I brought both hands up and touched my forehead with my fingers.

It looked like a total failure to connect because the cheerful woman triumphantly shouted, "You see?! You are unconsciously appealing to your inner god with that motion. You did THIS!" (She copied my hand movement.) Everyone laughed and nodded having caught me, a Christian, in a pagan motion indicating my "inner god" — not with my hands outstretched to the heavens in supplication to God. I had no idea the gesture had a particular meaning to them.

Dismayed, I protested, "No, no, no! I do THAT too, on my knees, my hands up, crying help with all my heart to God in heaven." I gestured, both hands in the air, palms up. Still, they laughed, and I did, too.

The cheerful woman concluded that the more of us who determine together to change, the more we really CAN change — ourselves, even the world. "Think of the study," she said, "Done on violent crime in the D.C. area in 1993. For two weeks 4,000 transcendental meditation experts meditated on peace, and the crime rate decreased by 18%." The thin man sounded hopeful: "So, we could have moved the tectonic plates, stopped the tsunami if enough of us meditated?" Many of them responded, "Yes!"

Then I heard a quiet voice. A tall woman (one of the organizers of the film festival) directly across from me who hadn't spoken the entire time softly said, "Bullshit." I clearly heard her, but others were asking, what did she say, what did she say? She gently repeated it, bull (pause) shit. Equal weight on both words.

It was a shock, a verbal tsunami. Everyone was silent for a minute. I began to softly laugh. Others joined in for other reasons, I suppose. The two-hour discussion was over.

One member of the group was a writer and invited me to get in touch with her. She wants to talk more about ideas of spirituality and mystery. But I'd definitely like to call the tall, one-word woman. Her summary was brilliant.

You Never Know

I NEED THESE ENCOUNTERS. My neighbors are real people battling pain, broken relationships, political tyranny, terrorism, and natural disasters. Their efforts to find peace disarmed my reluctance to listen to them, sitting there, as I did, without scripted answers. I understand more clearly their dead-end paths to salvation. No one wins heaven if in the end you are left on your own to fight the war against evil within and without. You can invoke spiritual power all you want, but in the end humans always lose. Even as a Christian, I'm familiar with this struggle. I've lost many times. The perfect beauty of the gospel is that God, in Christ, entirely gave himself to win that battle for us. That's what I wanted to tell them, but sometimes you only get half a shot. Perhaps their next encounter will be with Jonathan, and the Philistines of their lives will fall left and right. I pray so.

Toothpaste in the Toilet

WINTER 2012

"**D**UDE!! YOU NEED TO chill!"

I don't ordinarily talk like this, calling someone "Dude." It's pretentious for a woman my age. But it seemed appropriate at the time. I had to shout to get Denis' attention because he was flipping out.

He walked into the bedroom late one night and asked why there was water under the lid of the flip-top toothpaste container. When he opened it a bunch had spilled out. *Welll.* I remember thinking for a second: Margie, you need to lie here. Because you love him. But I couldn't think fast enough. I told the truth.

"I dropped it in the toilet."

Before I could assure him that I had washed it with hot water and soap, he was yelling; and what could I do? I hadn't thought of opening the lid to drain it. He was acting like he was going to be infected with a flesh eating bacteria or something.

I TOLD him there was nothing in the bowl, except water, and all you might get is a little pink-eye, ha-ha. (In case you don't know

— pink eye is caused by fecal contamination.)

He didn't think that was funny. As he went down the hall, he was still shouting, "WHAT were you thinking?" and et cetera.

A while later I got up to do something and saw he'd thrown away the toothpaste AND his toothbrush. So I had to ask, "What were YOU thinking? Like we can afford to throw away a perfectly good container of toothpaste? AND your toothbrush, too? What will all Ransom's donors think of being so wasteful? And after we told them how hard times were?"

I don't know whether I should report what he said, but it was: "And EVERY time I FIND that toothpaste back on the shelf I WILL throw it away."

So touchy! I told him *not* to touch it any more. The next day I bought him a new container of Crest. (I'll use up the old one myself.) The problem is that the new one looks exactly like the old one, and in a few weeks (until he reads this) he'll forget. And with our memory problems, well, you can see where this might lead.

UNHAPPILY, IN MY LIFE there are other categories of lost and fallen. To me, flying is like entering another dimension; you leave the airport in Minneapolis and arrive at Hogwart's Castle with body and mind intact. But when we flew to our annual board meeting in January, I lost my socks in that magical dimension. As we settled into our narrow little seats, I got hot. After adjusting the air, removing several layers of clothing, and still feeling frantic, I took off my shoes and socks, leaving them on the floor beside my computer case.

When we were about to land and I was re-dressing, I couldn't find my socks. Although we looked everywhere, they were gone. I decided not to worry because we landed in Phoenix where, what the hey, it's warm and my socks had holes in them anyway. But, still, I wonder, is it me? The universe? Or what?

Then there is my key-ring with front door, back door, storm door, and car keys that I *cannot* find. Unlike my cell phone which can be called from our landline to discover its location, I can't call my keys. So I retraced a week's worth of errands begging clerks and cashiers to check the Lost and Found. This happened while Denis was out of town with our car and I was borrowing Anita's second set of keys to drive *her* car. I thought mine were just bouncing around in my purse, apparently not. I thought about praying to find my keys until Denis showed me a *New Yorker* cartoon where an angel appears at the window of an overweight, disheveled-looking man, kneeling beside his bed and announces, "Your prayers are freaking God out." I'm freaking myself out.

Three Envies, Possibly More

IT MAY BE RISKING more to be honest about who I am, but what do I have to lose? I have more serious problems with breaking the 10th Commandment: "Thou shalt not covet." In an excellent book on his search for humility, Bruce Ray Smith writes:

> I admit to envy, a sin I deprecate in others and to which I had thought myself immune. Envy is a strain, a virulent strain, of pride: I should not be so surprised, so mortified to find myself infected.
>
> (*Winter Light*, Bruce Ray Smith, p.17)

So I admit to you that my envies include the following...

A writing retreat house. A sweet little cabin (designed by architect Andrew Berman) caught my attention because it was posted online. It is aesthetically gorgeous with calm colors and tidy shelves. A wide, clean desk faces a wall-sized window overlooking a sunny woods. Right now the ceiling of the office where I write is leaking. I was out running errands when my husband heard a rhythmic *plop, plop, plop-plop* and investigated. Water was dripping onto my bookshelves, open dictionary, and a stack of papers. The ceiling is now drooping and stained the color of tobacco juice. Then I recalled a writer who wrote every day from a tiny desk jammed into her small, dark closet that smelled like an old shoe.

I have a window that looks out on a luxurious linden tree. I have a small tapestry that softens the wall above my desk. The floor is honeyed-colored fir, and my messy L-shaped desk is large enough to host a sweet collection of giraffes. The bathroom is right next door. Bonus!

A successful nonprofit organization. I admired the way this organization celebrated their 20th anniversary this past year. When I heard that a couple of crack chefs were coming from far away to help cook a feast for the attendees, I blushed. What? Why didn't Ransom do something like that for our 20th anniversary? Back then, Denis thought of splurging on a roll of *foil stickers* we could place on envelopes announcing: Celebrating 20 Years! But wait, wasn't this our own failure of imagination? We had no energy or ambition to do more. Should friends be faulted for doing what they do so well — mentoring and launching gifted musicians and artists? Ransom's 30th anniversary is coming up next year. So. Margie? Never mind, I get where this is going.

Friends who took a trip to France. This couple sent secret waves of envy through my heart. During grape harvest? Fromage fests? Café crème on the plaza? They are precious friends who have hosted us many times and spent countless hours loving us through dark and fainting times. And last November, didn't I get, not only what what I needed, but just what I wanted, after all? A quiet place on a lake without television or neighbors. A fireplace, windows to the sun, books, coffee and a good companion. Yes, I did.

TRYING TO TALK MYSELF out of every envy I feel doesn't seem to work, even though I don't want to be that kind of person. I'd like you to think I'm better than that; kinder, more generous. But even *that* is a deceitful desire fueled by pride. What God has in mind is something radical and painful, a deeper magic — the stripping of my walls down to the studs. He wants to remake me.

Again, Smith's honesty forces me to admit where I am:

I want to be cured of the ills with which my pride afflicts me. But even without them, even freed from isolation, contempt and self-contempt, I will be no better. I still won't know how to live; I won't know, not here nor in heaven, how to be until I learn who I am, who I am now and who God meant, means, me to be.

(*Winter Light*, p. 22.)

Self-Centered Prayers Get a Little Help

I FORGOT MY ANGLICAN prayer beads on the window sill at the cabin in Wisconsin. A friend had made them from beautiful gemstones of jade and onyx. I sat at the window for morning prayer, looking out on the sky and lake, the chickadees darting to the feeder, snatching sunflower seeds. A great spot for contemplation. In the past, I would have gasped if you had suggested I use prayer beads. I thought they were as pagan as witches and Stonehenge. Repeating mumbled words. Fingering beads — idolatry! Useless at best.

I was wrong. Perhaps it's my age, but I think I could have used their help a long time ago. Now, I'm sorry they will need to be replaced. I've always needed help with focus and clarity. My mind strays. No, that's not true; it doesn't just stray, without an anchor it entirely sails away on the smallest puff of wind. My prayers are far too self-centric. They focus on my needs, my wants. "Dear God, help me be a better person so people will like me. Heal my body. Give me a fun time. Give me safety when I travel. Help me find spare change for coffee, and make my pillows soft." If I have time to spare, I might pray for my husband and anyone close who is having a big problem.

To oppose this inclination to make self the center of the universe, I use the four sections of seven beads each to help me pray in other ways for other people, with other needs than my own:

Prayers for others — I can't begin to pray for all the needs of all people around the world, but in a finite way, I can pray for some. I often pray for unmarried friends because I don't think it's easy being either single or celibate in the culture of the American church. For people suffering under tyranny, war and famine, I ask God to spare and comfort them. I remind myself we have a God who sees them all, and I, too, am comforted.

Prayers for family — immediate family. There are always things to remember or give thanks for. Despite what we may present to the world, who has a family that isn't facing difficulty in some way? So sometimes a particular bead represents a particular person.

Prayers for self — seven whole beads for all my confessions, causes and worries.

Prayers of thanksgiving and praise — for bringing his words to us through Scripture. For the men and women who wrote them down and were willing to belong to him with all their great and pitiful lives, who were human and flawed, like me. For God being not one, but Trinity. I use that language: thanks be to the Father, Son and Holy Ghost.

The beads begin and end with the cross. And so, too, my prayers. I want to live, try to live, with this in mind — that God's plan is to restore all things via the cross. That plan includes me. By it, one day, I'll be resurrected and renewed, and then I'll never drop the toothpaste in the toilet or lose my keys or slam a door. Nor will I envy, ever again.

POSTSCRIPT: I ORDERED A new set of prayer beads from the *Solitaries of de Koven*. They're made of African jasper beads; their earthy colors remind me that I, and those I love, are made of dust, and yet our days are numbered by a creator who loves his children and will take us Home some day. There are many ways to use the Anglican prayer beads as an assist to prayer and meditation. Nothing sacred about how Margie does it.

Distorting to Fit
FALL 2013

Wrench |renCH|

Verb [with obj.]

~ pull or twist (someone or something) suddenly and violently...

~ injure (a part of the body) as a result of a sudden twisting movement...

~ turn with a wrench...

~ *archaic* distort to fit a particular theory or interpretation...

---

*T*ODAY I WRENCHED MYSELF. I wonder what to make of it. Sometimes writing down the details helps a story sort itself out and you begin to gain insight: Oh, this is about this. Or that. Perhaps that will happen this afternoon. I have a vague notion there may be misconceptions that twist my heart. Perhaps I've distorted life to fit a particular theory...

I left for the mall this morning after a meeting with Marcy,

Ransom's bookkeeper. It had to be a quick stop on my way to the bank. After my business at at the mall, I quickly headed for the car. Looking up and down the row, I could not see our car anywhere. What?! I pressed the panic button on my keys, but didn't hear a horn blaring. I stood puzzled. These are frightening moments for people my age. Our brains begin frantically beeping. Red alert! Red alert! And worse than the brain not finding a reasonable explanation is when it finds nothing at all. Nothing to calm the heart.

I usually remember where I park by recalling the direction I was headed when I found an empty spot — was I pointed toward the entrance or away? I knew it was toward. Wasn't it? I looked in the next row, but the car wasn't there either. Or the next. Or the next.

About that time, a woman getting out of her SUV stopped to ask if I'd lost my car. Was my wandering *that* obvious? Embarrassed, I admitted yes. She sympathetically recalled, I did that just last week. Looked everywhere. Couldn't remember where I'd parked.

What color is your car? Dark blue, Ford 500. Why it's right there! she pointed. No, that's a Chevrolet. Shall I drive you around? I can do that. Why don't I? No, no, it's okay, it's got to be right here somewhere.

By then I was ready to call Denis to report our car had been stolen. Really, the lady insisted, I can take you. This was too much kindness; I had to refuse. I should be the one showing kindness to strangers, *not* receiving it. *I* am self-sufficient.

She finally left me alone in a desert of cars and walked toward the doors. Complete in my humiliation, I looked up at the sky, and that was when, through some kind of electrifying nerve-burst, (God? Holy Spirit?) I remembered I had driven Anita's car, not our own. And her car happened to be the one sitting right in front of me. I gave a loud groan (I may have cussed) and the lady who was still within earshot hollered, Did you find it? Did you find it?! Then I had to explain that I had forgotten I'd borrowed a car....

This does not really *explain*, though, does it?

Twisting the Wrench

I HEADED TO THE bank in a greater hurry to get back home because I have big, important writing deadlines and should be putting words on paper right this second. As I came out, I passed Marcy on her way into the bank with a Ransom deposit. I waved and smiled.

Outside, I stopped and thought, why, Margie, you could save her a trip back to our house if you waited a minute for the receipts. That was when I turned around to run back in, tripped on the curb and fell face down. I could attribute this tumble to the achy joints I'd been nursing all week, but again, I don't think that entirely *explained* what was happening either.

For what seemed like hours, I lay on the sidewalk. More humiliation. Why did God allow this? (God is remarkably patient with unjustified blame.) My knee felt exploded, my wrist hurt and I had managed to hit my lip on the sidewalk. Our bank is a very quiet place and not a soul came in or out, nor did a car drive past as I finally pulled myself to a sitting position and sat thinking that if anyone *did* come along and express the smallest degree of sympathy I would begin sobbing. No. I'd wail. Loud, mournful howls. With more groaning, I hoisted myself up and hobbled to the car.

I'm home now. Working from bed. I was planning on having what I call a "Bed Day" anyway, because I need a little extra time for recovery from recent travels. Now that my fall has added more body parts to the problem, I wonder how to get everything done that needs doing. I've received plenty of sympathy here at home. Denis teases me saying I should begin using a walker (right, dude) but he has brought me ice tea, my cell phone, and a pillow. Anita says she'll make lunch. (She made supper, too.)

Distorting to Fit

THAT MORNING, I HAD awakened early from a fitful night of not sleeping. Denis *seemed* awake when I asked him about a dilemma I was pondering: I need to finish writing the next issue of *Notes From Toad Hall* and it takes hours of concentrated writing. There is no way I'll make the deadline on Saturday.

The problem is we are planning to go away for two nights this weekend. (Days off are difficult to manage at home because Toad Hall is also our work, where our offices are located. Work is everywhere and cries to us. From the basement to the attic we hear it calling "Emails, emails, emails! Phone call! Doorbell, doorbell! Read me, read me." Sometimes we are compelled to go away to get downtime.)

I thought of three options for dealing with my deadline:

1. Simply look at the days as time off for *Denis'* sake. I would go along, but keep working.
2. Limit self to 3 hours of work each day and let the remaining hours be time off the grid.
3. Or just believe you need this time away, too. Kick your schedule in the butt. You made it up yourself, anyway, not some CEO who threatens your life.

With half his brain intact, Denis mumbles, "Number three," and falls back asleep.

I decided to give my word and stick with it. But I tell you, it's not easy. My being, my life, my brain are programmed to kill self before giving up. I am a responsible, committed, dependable, hard-working wretch and God forbid someone should find me floating on an air mattress in some lake somewhere.

I know, that's a little sick. But what can I do?

Maybe THAT is what the morning was about? I *wrench* myself and finally hear a message? Fall down, rack my knee, hobble around with a walking stick, and am forced to go to bed immediately after supper, because I erroneously think I need to save the world and fix every little whatever?

God is speaking to me from the parking lot of a mall, from the sidewalk in front of the bank. The unmistakable message is YOU CAN'T save the world. That's MY job.

To be honest, I need some help. Professional help. Not that I've ever had a problem with *others* getting counseling — but as for me? I've always felt we couldn't afford the cost or the time or the shame of me being such a needy person.

Now that I'm seeing someone, I'm sorry I waited so long. I was all prepared to understand how my spouse's problems affect me and how if he changed, then I'd get all better. But when the first thing this counselor suggested is that I read a book called *Boundaries: When to say yes, how to say no to take control of your life* by Cloud & Townsend, I groaned, "awwwwww." I've heard about that book forever, but was quite sure it was full of advice I already knew, but I dutifully ordered it because I am, after all, Responsible-Oldest-Child and wish to please everyone.

Taking care of yourself by saying "no, I can't" is a troublesome thought to those who want to follow Christ whatever the cost and will bleed from every orifice in order to prove it. It is also troublesome for those of us who see that our current culture basically encourages everyone to be efficiently self-indulgent, self-focused, and to never restrict our pleasure.

Early in our marriage when Denis and I were young and rather ill-advised, we sold everything we had, gave away all our money *and* our car in order to prove we wanted to be good disciples of Jesus. This, I now see, was not exactly God's requirement. We were idealistic and had no idea how to follow God with every ounce of our being unless we gave ground to every need that stirred our hearts.

Touching Others after All

As I READ THE book and tried to listen with unbiased ears, every so often it hit a homerun.

> ...Don't boundaries turn us from other-centeredness to self-cen-teredness? The answer is no. *Appropriate boundaries actually increase our ability to care about others.*

What Christ calls us to isn't the same thing as saying yes to everyone and everything.

> Self-care is never a selfish act — it is simply good stewardship of the only gift I have, the gift I was put on earth to offer to others. Anytime we can listen to true self and give it the care it requires, we do so not only for ourselves but for the many others whose lives we touch.

(Parker Palmer, *Let Your Life Speak*)

My brain must contain years of neurological entrenchment and an archive full of boundary violations. I don't know when to stop worrying about other people. Some of the more pressing questions are: "if I don't, who will? What will so-and-so think of me if I don't? I'm afraid I won't be loved. Why did I start this pattern? Where does this trouble come from?"

Perhaps one beginning: as a child I was obsessed with anxiety about our house burning down. When my parents were gone and I was babysitting my five younger brothers and sisters, I constantly worried about them. It was bitter cold outside and our front door was frozen shut. How would I get them all out the back door if a fire started? I repeatedly checked the gas burners on the kitchen stove and warily watched our wood stove glow red hot.

As I SAT ON the hot pavement after falling in front of the bank; it suddenly occurred to me; Marcy needed to come back to our house *anyway*, so *what* was I thinking?! Well, I *think* that for years I've been following a path of trying to rescue people from their house fires, even if they're not real.

This is not what Christ requires of me. He often left the multitudes and all their needs behind for various reasons. This path is my own, designed to relieve my own fears. It's more about myself than others and that smarts.

LEARNING TO SAY NO even to good things so we can say yes to what God has called us to do is scary and requires clarification. It poses lots of questions. What *ought* we to be doing? How *do* we take care of ourselves properly? Does it include rest and play? What about real suffering around us?

I can't fit everything together yet, but I'm listening with expectation.

I feel like I have a rare chance to change at an age when I am prone to calcification. I can still to grow into a fuller understanding of the gospel of Christ and that really sparks my heart.

Toad Hall

Taod Hall at Christmas

Toad Hall — front walk

Toad Hall — winter

1979: Jerem & baby Sember

1989: Denis & Margie

Bobblehead Jesus oversees the sink at Toad Hall

Consider Jesus — grandchildren's favorite
ornament, "Jesus in the nest"

Toad Hall kitchen

Toad Hall dining room

Toad Hall back porch (where Honeysuckle lived)

Little Manassah "stolen away" from school

Margie & Sember — "done parenting"

"Skirting the fleece" with Anita Gorder

2014: Ava Lou "washes" the dishes

1952: Grandpa Frolander & Margie

Mountain Ash tree berries at Toad Hall

Neighbor Susan's yard

Toad Hall back yard, sheets drying in the sun

Toad Hall living room — Steve Garber & Margie

Toad Hall Living Room

Toad Hall living room

Mole's End

2014: Margie & Denis

I Want What the Cat Ate

SPRING 2004

IN A SMALL TOWN near Rochester, a man driving his van along a river saw a bald eagle swoop down and grab a sixteen inch sucker from the water. Larry Knight slowed to watch, "I thought it was really awesome to watch an eagle fly into the creek and pick a fish up," he said.

The eagle struggled to gain altitude with the extra weight. You know, after an eagle grabs a fish it quickly adjusts its hold so the fish slices through the air, decreasing the drag. (I learned this from David Attenborough's "Life of Birds" video series. It's very, very cool how they grasp it along the spine with one claw in front of the other.) It's apparently not so easy to mount up on wings of an eagle when you're trying to shift a slapping, slippery fish.

This eagle lost its grip as it ascended over the top of Larry's van. The dropped fish shattered his windshield and exploded guts and fish eggs over the front of the van. Larry says the van is now sitting in his driveway because the insurance company claims they don't cover damage from flying fish. He also reports that the neighbor's cat ate what was left on the vehicle. He decided the next time he sees an eagle carrying a fish he won't be stopping to watch, "I'm givin' her the gas," he said.

At first, I thought one might identify with the driver: you stop to admire God's creation, thinking that by it you will gain a deeper understanding of God, but as you draw near, his handiwork contrives to injure you. You are struck by the apparent random nature of misfortune and God's irrational plan for your spiritual growth — like when, for the first time as an adult, you decide to give your self completely to Christ, and the next two years are the worst of your life.

In just a small illustration of how this works in my life: on a recent morning my partner decided he was going to be the best husband that day, and it wasn't even Mother's Day or my birthday. It was just a day in which he was going to demonstrate his love by taking me to dinner and a movie. And me? Even though I belong to God, body and soul, by noon I'd crossed him five times, called him a name, and sold his favorite chair.

Then I thought, perhaps the eagle serves as the main point here; he scores high for trying. It didn't work out this time, but he's not going to stop fishing. So I'm the eagle, I've caught the fish, and, yes, I've dropped it, and made a big mess; however, I'm not giving up. Remember, "You will soar on wings like eagles?" (Isaiah 40:31). It's the verb that defines when success happens. "You will" is future tense. So what if I'm not quite mounting up on wings today. So what if I've lost the prize fish? Tomorrow, or, at the very least, in the next life, I will be more like Jesus, so I will keep on longing to fly, I will keep fishing, because one day I'm going to carry that damn fish back to my nest and eat it.

In the end, it isn't the driver *or* the eagle I fully appreciate in this allegory of life. It's the cat. Imagine him on the same old, same old stealth inspection. On his rounds to the back door, the flower pots, the roll-away trash bin. Just a routine, ordinary night out marking his territory. Suddenly he sniffs the surprising odor of fish eggs and guts wafting off the hood of a van. (Never mind how unlikely the spot, God often reveals himself on detours. Think about Moses turning aside to investigate the burning bush.) There, amidst shards of glass is the most unexpected and exquisite of pleasures — sucker roe. He leaps up, his pink tongue and needle teeth pulling away sacs and veins (it's a dangerous feast, but, oh, so worth it); it is Christ, beckoning us from among the broken flower pots and trash bins, come dine with me. I want to be the cat.

Parsing the Prepositional Phrase

I WOULD LIKE MY soul feasting on something nourishing with Jesus, but I'm in a spiritual funk. As I trudge through my daily rounds, to the kitchen, to the store, to the office, I'm keeping an eye out for some word, some thing that will move me out of the desert, out of the routine and ordinary. In my search, I came across a quote from Eugene Peterson which appeared in *Context* (published by Martin Marty). I have a sinking feeling that Peterson knows me:

First, Christian spirituality, the contemplative life, is not about us. It is about God. The great weakness of American spirituality is that it is all about us: fulfilling our potential, getting the blessings of God, expanding our influence, finding our gifts, getting a handle on principles by which we can get an edge over the competition. The more there is of us, the less there is of God. Christian spirituality is not a life-project for becoming a better person. It is not about developing a so-called deeper life. We are in on it, to be sure, but we are not the subject. Nor are we the action. We get included by means of a few prepositions: God with us (Matt. 1:23), Christ in me (Gal. 2:20), God for us (Rom. 8:31). With, in, for: They are powerful, connecting, relation-forming words, but none of them makes us either the subject or the predicate. We are the tag-end of a prepositional phrase.

Sooner or later in this life we get invited or commanded to do something. But in that doing, we never become the subject of the Christian life nor do we perform the action of the Christian life. We are invited or commanded into what I call prepositional participation. The prepositions that join us to God and God's action in us within the world – the with, the in, the for – are very important, but they are essentially a matter of the ways and means of being in on and participating in what God is doing.

(Eugene Peterson)

It occurred to me that as much as I don't want to be influenced by American cultural details which run counter to spirituality, I am American. I'm prone to the cowboy attitude of I-can-do-anything by myself, and all of life is about me. I breathe American air. I process American news which shows a city employee rescuing eight baby ducklings who fell into the storm sewer beside the photo of a Palestinian father lying on the ground cradling his screaming daughter during an Israeli attack, and then I plan an American supper. I hear him.

I'm dead in a spiritual desert.

Unexpected Revelations

HAVE YOU EVER TRIED another favorite American remedy for depression and spiritual dryness? Shopping? I thought I could purchase a little cheap help with an item which was described in the following way: (See if you can guess what I bought.)

When you want to keep [Blank 1] close to your [Blank 2], keep it in your pocket. It's easy with the [Blank 3]. This highly portable [Blank 4] slips into your pocket or purse with room to spare. It's ideal for plane trips, day hikes, lunch with a friend, or anywhere you've ever found yourself wishing you had a [Blank 4] conveniently at hand.

Did you figure it out? A battery operated screwdriver from Menards? Maybe a new Hi-Protein Power Bar with chocolate and blueberries? Or it could a Global Positioning Device, because it sounds like the target buyer is pretty mobile. Well, no surprise, none of the above. Here's the key:

Blank 1 = God's Word

Blank 2 = heart

Blank 3 = NIV Trimline New Testament with Psalms and Proverbs

Blank 4 = Bible

I didn't even notice the shameful copy on the outside back cover until I had owned this unique little New Testament for a couple of months and was thinking of sending a copy to Jeremy Huggins, a writer friend who used to have a blog called *Junk Mail for Blankets.* One of his posts was titled "an unscripted prayer for mercy," a reflection on what and why Bible reading is so dead hard (cannily knowing that many of us struggle with it, but few Christians dare to admit it) He concludes the piece with "Here's what it comes down to. I know I need my Bible. But I don't know exactly why. And deep in my heart's script, I catch myself thinking that I was doing alright before he came along, showing him with my non-Bible-reading that I don't need his approval. I'll just sit outside and play with fire. Sure, God says I need the Bible, but I don't see it — what, do you think you own this place, that you're the Boss of me? God forbid. Please. God forbid me."

This post drew a lot of discussion and confession among his readers. It caused me to face, once again, my own habits and difficulties with reading the Bible. The reason I bought the New Testament in the first place, was because I thought my problem was that I needed a change from the ugly, cheap edition of a new Bible translation I've been trying to read through. This Zondervan New Testament appealed to me, because it's small (three inches by six), it's a nice color (creamed coffee, I'd call it), and it feels nice (smooth and glossy). It seems like such weakness to admit that when I'm thirsty and dry with spiritual deadness, I buy a new edition of the Bible, as if ordering a triple espresso at Starbucks when I need an energy jolt is a healthy thing to do (although I do it anyway). After I read the back cover, I not only felt more defeated, I now felt angry and stupid. I'd joined the marketing-for-Jesus forces I despise. "This highly portable Trimline New Testament with Psalms and Proverbs slips into your pocket with room to spare!" Sadly, this created unnecessary cynicism in me and I wondered if it could cause some to doubt the seriousness of the scriptures.

God's Word is life to me. I spend time in it because it changes me in a mysterious way. The fact that merely reading it subtly changes me has been at times a source of irritation, and something I don't like to acknowledge because in addition to a lot of other problems, I am prideful. But the people who know me best, because they have lived with me — my mother, my husband — say they know when I neglect this spiritual discipline. It is not inspiring to be so congenitally ill-natured. However, there are plenty of times when I despair of ever reading the Bible again. Nothing resonates, nothing strikes. And when I've lost the sense of the reality of God in my life, I am deaf to all platitudes and preachiness. So don't tell me "faith follows action like the little caboose on the train."

What I'm experiencing is spiritual dryness, and my first instinct is to do exactly what Tim Keller describes in a sermon on Psalm 42. He says that when something goes wrong for American Christians, they look for someone or some thing to pin it on. We tend to be very moralistic and think that surely, spiritual dryness is the result of unconfessed sin in our life. We haven't pushed the right button, we've neglected our Christian "to-do list."

What we need to grasp, he says, is that dryness is going to happen no matter where, who, or how old you are as a Christian. It isn't necessarily because you've done something wrong, or haven't had faith, or neglected to read through the Bible in a year. It's because you're human and we live in a fractured, fallen world.

Keller examines Psalm 42 which reflects the nature of our disorder. The psalmist asks "Why are you downcast, O my soul? Why are you so disturbed?" The question is not rhetorical; it isn't at all cynical, or sarcastic. It is actually asking us for self-examination. So the psalmist searches for hopes. What are they? Where are they? That's when I understood my own hopes: I've misplaced them in people who have failed me or in plans that fell through, in things that broke, in things that can never be.

When the big hopes fail I concentrate on little things in life: When can Margie have a latte? When can she eat some chocolate? When can she sit in the sun, listen to music, read a good story, write a punchy status update? Making "Self" my integrative personal center has been profoundly disappointing, because in and of themselves things can't sustain my soul for very long either. So the psalmist declares a shift: "Hope in God," he tells himself. And he begins to think about *"chesed"* — the Hebrew word for God's loving-kindness and covenant-keeping. The psalmist recounts his personal history and all the times God helped him, and since he is a professional musician and a poet, he turns the grace of God into a song he sings to himself through the night: "By day the Lord directs his love, at night his song is with me."

I had no idea this psalm would administer a powerful grace at the just the right time.

Eat Your Fish Eggs. Yummy.

LAST WEEK AS I was updating the calendar and thinking nothing more could fit into that week, we got an early morning phone call. At first, all I heard were stifled sobs and sniffling. As soon as I determined it was most likely our five-year-old granddaughter, I relaxed a little. It wasn't the dreaded call announcing someone you love has been killed in a car accident. It was Manessah and she wanted to talk. She'd just awakened from a bad dream and couldn't shake it. She'd been to the zoo with her little friend, Gracey, and inexplicably found herself alone on a bus to Rochester, but she couldn't find our house. She felt like I was lost from her. You know that nightmarish feeling when you urgently need to reach someone and you can't? On the phone she said, "I need to see you because we are moving very far away and I won't see you very often anymore." It's true, they are moving to Tennessee.

At the time, I was in the process of writing an issue of *Notes From Toad Hall*. It was due at the printer and I hadn't even gotten it to our layout editor yet, so I was really late. We weigh these things, don't we? What is more important? What trumps this or that? Especially, how do we manage deadlines that pit them against the needs of those we love? Sometimes the person who really needs you can't tell you. I noticed this about our children, and I continue to see it in the children of our friends. Adult obligations, meetings, appointments appear so pressing and important, even older children know they can't say, couldn't you drop that meeting? Just stay home and do nothing? Hang out with me in case I think of something important like where's my allowance, or what would you think if I got a tattoo? That sort of being present with someone means: don't invite anyone else to join you, don't answer the phone, and especially, don't do email or texting.

This was one choice that was pretty easy to make. The next day

I left the office behind — with its unanswered letters and unfinished writing. I drove to Minneapolis, snuck Manessah out of school, and took her to a really cool children's bookstore, The Wild Rumpus, where they have cats curled up in easy chairs, and real live chickens wandering around. I'm serious. We looked at books, had an ice cream cone at an old fire station-turned-shop. Things could wait until the next day. And they did.

Sometimes when we set aside what appears to be costly time to be with someone, we imagine it will be historic. We imagine the slaking of our spiritual thirst will involve something epic like a voice from heaven. Some of us think it might include the sharing of unforgettable music, food, books, and conversation so deep life will never be the same. But this is how it actually was for my spiritually shriveled little soul: the day was mild and sunny, and the waves on Lake Calhoun were very blue, as Manessah pointed out. At The Wild Rumpus, the little white hen with feathers on her feet (who allows you to pet her) laid an egg on the floor under a bookshelf, and Manessah picked it up while it was still warm. We bought *Ramona, the Pest* by Beverly Cleary, ate lunch at McDonald's capping it off with a McFlurry. She sang the names of the continents to the tune of "Twinkle, Twinkle Little Star." The conversation that drifted from the back seat of the car was not profound:

"I'm hungry, can we get a cheeseburger? I would love the puppy they give with Happy Meals."

"I wonder if people will think you're my mother?"

"Probably not. I'm a bit older than your mother."

Quietly, to herself: "That's right. She has white hair, and she's very, very, very old."

When I left, she hugged me tight and thanked me for "stoling" her away from school. I promised that when they moved, I would write her, call her, and we would visit them in Tennessee. What she gave me was surely more than I gave to her. We had a just-right, ordinary, every-day time.

So I'm back with the cat who discovered fish eggs on the van. There are no reliable predictors for where you'll find a feast or what person will become your drink in the desert. Or what Scripture God may use to give you hope for that day. This morning I read "I do not concern myself with great matters or things too wonderful for me. But I have calmed and quieted my soul; like a weaned child with its mother, like a weaned child is my soul within me. O, Israel, put your hope in the Lord both now and forever more" (Ps. 131:1–2).

I think I hear what David is saying, since I know a little about weaning babies. A nursing baby can disturb an entire urban neighborhood with her demands. Because of this, her demands are generally met as quickly as possible any time of the day or night. A weaned child has learned to wait. She knows she'll be fed eventually. She doesn't quiz her mom about organic food standards as the sweet potatoes are mashed, nor does she ask if her mom understands debit card payments at Hyvee. She just sits in her highchair patiently watching and waiting while her mother prepares her food. And when the food is finally ready she eats.

Parenting with Snakes
JUNE 1990

*L*AST WINTER I BOUGHT a small trailer for not much money. As they say in Minnesota: it was not too baduva deal. It is the kind that is good for hauling furniture, large Christmas trees, and trash. I also knew it would come in handy if we ever cleaned out our attic, basement and garage. That day came this spring.

Jerem, Sember and I began the process. We hauled out glass jars, old carpets, kerosene heaters, a broken black-and-white TV set, old doors, scrap lumber, broken suitcases, and 27 metal venetian blinds. The garage was plugged and the trailer buried when Denis got home from his last trip. That was only the beginning. We still had about 100 square yards of cardboard boxes full of plastic peanuts sitting in the attic. Don't ask.

Denis took one look around and turned a shade of gray. The garage wasn't just a mess of my junk collections — our kids had contributed to the chaos with stacks of undelivered newspapers, old bike parts, and worn sports equipment. As he began throwing things in the trailer, I suggested we'd better think the whole thing through, in other words, how were we going to organize. So he paused, hands on hips. "Why would you organize trash?"

I took a breath and explained that I had called the County Recycling Center and each trailer load would cost us $12.75 — that's if it contained metal or burnables such as wood and plastic, but if the load did not contain all of one type of trash, when we got there we would have to sort it out there, and since they recycled cardboard, we didn't have to pay for that or newspapers, on the other hand, they would pay us for glass and aluminum so we may as well sort here.

Denis scowled and began throwing wood on top of the cardboard in the trailer. "Just a minute!" I cried. "We don't want to mix up that space. Since they charge us for wood — why put in cardboard? Unless we have a whole trailer full of it and make a separate trip?"

"So just *how* do you want me to do this?" Denis asked. I proposed we could do it however he decided was best since he now had all the facts.

We stood quietly awaiting his decision except for Sember who was sweeping up choking clouds of dust from the floor. The minutes dragged on while Denis looked more and more irritated. I began thinking: "Oh, yes. This is a typical Haack Family Work Day. So much fun."

(I started rolling my eyes a little. Not a lot. Just quiet little rolls. But Denis didn't miss that small movement.)

Finally, Denis emptied out the cardboard. "We'll fill it with the other stuff first."

He picked up a heavy box of old paint cans to heave in the trailer, and I yelled, "No! Not THAT! Sorry, I forgot to mention. Hazardous waste. That can't be mixed in with the anything else. They only accept that on Saturday mornings between eight and noon. And one other thing, they'll take the old tires, but that will cost us extra."

Dropping the box with a crash, eyes bulging slightly, he picked up a plastic bag full of grass clippings and plants. I so hated to say, but I had to tell him he was holding compostable material and that couldn't be mixed in with anything else, either. However, we could get rid of it for free if we hauled it to the city's compost pile.

By then I was beginning to wonder why someone as intelligent as my husband could not organize a few little trips to the dump. I was becoming irritated myself and more than a little impatient. Now Denis was snapping at us, Jerem was heaving big meaningful sighs and Sember continued on in oblivion. (Every family needs someone like her. She was a wonderful antidote for family tension. As long as she was able to focus, she could forge ahead with good humor, ignoring the stress around her, humming merrily as she worked.)

My philosophy of work is similar to the Seven Dwarves in Disney's *Snow White*. You remember how they got their jobs done? Quickly! No complaining! In no time at all with cooperation, smiles, willing hands, all the while singing "Whistle While You Work." Ha-ha. I know this isn't reality any more now than it was back in the Depression when that movie was made. Still it is my inherent weakness to expect it from my family.

That afternoon God reminded me of another reason why family projects often don't work around here. I had lately been contemplating a phrase from I Corinthians 13: "Love is not easily provoked." Not easily provoked. Case in point. I *am* easily provoked. Guess who provokes me the most easily? Denis. The person I love most in the world, am most committed to. He provokes me. Most of the time it is over some small thing.

I was convicted by my lack of patience — my failure to see, through his eyes, the chaotic, complicated mess we had created in the garage. I was convicted by my surly response to his stress, not that he couldn't have used some extra patience of his own. What was more distressing was the speed at which I can move from eager-beaver work projects to door-slamming, box-kicking anger.

Love is patient. Love is kind. *Love is not easily provoked.* It stays calm. It explains patiently. Love might even consider the stress of re-entering the family dynamic after you've been on the road for days at a time working at your calling and you need time to recover. It also considers the impact of the smallest eye-roll.

There is no way I can do this. The only chance I have for changing is if God helps me carry my burdens inch by painful inch.

It took much longer than I had planned, but we finally got a load ready and hauled it to the Recycle Center.

Snake-Handling in the Home

AFTER THREE YEARS OF drought, spring rains were heavy and welcome this year. They deeply drenched the lawn, soaked the trees and caused our tulips to blaze. The snakes must have appreciated the rains because they hatched in greater numbers. Sember found a long green garter snake in our front yard and screamed for me to come the other day. They are harmless — we only have the harmless kinds in most of Minnesota (not counting the few timber rattlers that live in the river bluffs). I grabbed it by the tail and we watched, fascinated while it made esses in the air.

It was the sort of thing that brought back memories. My brother and I sometimes collected a basketful of garter snakes, holding the lid down tight while we took them out one by one, we pinned them to the clothesline amid the white sheets that billowed in the sun. We would hide behind an old stock tank and watch as our unsuspecting mother came out to gather in the laundry. Her shrieks of surprise delighted us as unpinned snakes fell writhing into her clothesbasket. She was hard to scare and probably faked it for our sakes.

Sember and I decided that the snake had too much potential to pass up. What fun it would be to surprise someone with a snake! So we waited until Jerem came home from school and headed for the bathroom. Although none of our bathrooms have locks on the doors, we have never bothered to install them because it is our policy to not disturb anyone's privacy when the door is closed. Sember and I slipped quietly up the stairs, slowly cracked the door, and released the writhing reptile. We were rewarded by loud shrieks and thumps that told us he was jumping into the tub. Fortunately Jerem is a pretty good sport and decided immediately that he ought to pass this favor on to his dad. (Denis was in New Jersey at the time.)

Denis has such a phobia of snakes that I hesitated to let Jerem release it in our bed — like he wanted — or even to drop it on his lap as he read the newspaper. I was truly afraid he might have a heart attack. Anyway, it was all for nothing because we forgot to hide the snake's cage and the normally unobservant Denis walked in the door from the airport and spotted it instantly. So Jerem simply waved it in Denis' face, which was almost as good as releasing it in the bathroom.

Perhaps the best response was when Sember greeted her friend Rachel in the backyard. All she did was hold its weaving body with its red tongue flicking her in the face and Rachel bent double and screamed for five excruciating minutes. This is no exaggeration. Neighbors ran to their windows and workmen in the neighborhood paused to look in our back yard to see if someone had died.

Why do we enjoy doing this sort of thing? It seems that not only am I easily provoked, I enjoy provoking others. Love ought to make me sensitive about crossing the line from okay joking to provoking.

Not too long ago, I had a day when I ran out of energy and health before my daily work was done. Jerem came home from school and saw me resting on the couch amid piles of laundry. He took one look, pivoted on his heel and was gone. He was soon back leading Denis from the office. Jerem announced that I was not to move — he and Dad were going to fix dinner and it was all his idea. Jerem had even planned the menu.

Deeply touched, I whispered, "Jerem, this is so kind of you. You don't know how much I appreciate this."

"Aw, it's okay, Mom," he responded. "I took one look at you and knew that if we were going to have any dinner at all I'd have to fix it myself and I happen to be very hungry."

I sank back. So much for altruistic motives. I laughed at the irony because it reminded me of how much I do that is sustained by selfish motives — especially if there is an audience to witness it. Trying to look good to others is just another part of the sinful brew in my heart. It can be disheartening, enough to want to give up, but that is no answer either. It seems God desires us to keep going while being mindful of our condition: this is who we are: incomplete works, broken, in need of repair, but recipients of grace. Paul says God has *lavished* grace on us and that he receives us and forgives us. Lavish means extravagant – completely, generously buttered, edge to edge. (Eph. 1:7–8) Thank God for a grace that says, yes, I see your hateful attitude toward your husband, and I still lavish you. Thank God for grace that says you almost stopped your son's heart so you could have a laugh, and I still pour it on. I love you.

Our menu that night was very good — a bit light on the leafy greens, but I wasn't complaining about venison chops, Greek flatbread, corn, and Jello with whipped cream. No.

Joy in Unexpected Places
CHRISTMAS 2005

ONE REASON I THINK God made children is because they're gifted at making spontaneous joy in the midst of some pretty startling circumstances. Jeremy Huggins once reported on his blog *Junkmail For Blankets* that he was visiting a friend whose "two-year-old girl vomited all over the table where I was sitting. She looked down at the vomit, looked up at me, laughed, and said, 'Jeremy, I frowed up.'" Jeremy is not a father. Which, strangely, increased the irony and the humor of this, don't you think?

Although I can't trump a child having spontaneous joy over such a strange thing, I can recall a few random stories that might amuse you for a moment or two.

My Aunt Beatty Frolander, who was as Swedish as a meatball, fondly called my mother a "dumb Svede," even though Mom is not a blonde, and even though last fall she shot a buck from her bathroom window. (This doesn't mean as her daughter I'm a crack shot or as good-looking, but it does make me Scandinavian, which means I get to tell my people's jokes.)

At Farmer's Market last fall, Denis and I overheard a grizzled Norwegian tell this to a circle of old guys who slapped their thighs in appreciation: Sven, Ole, and his wife, Lena, were ice fishing on a little lake in Minnesota. After they fished awhile, Ole asks Lena if she'd walk across the lake over there to Johnson's bait shop and buy him some beef jerky, don't you know. She says, "Ya, I s'pose I will. Do you have any money?" Ole says, "No but you can just put it on my account there, then." They watched her walk about half a mile across the ice, and Sven finally says, "Ole, how come you didn't give her some cash, I know you got some there in your pocket? Ole replied, "I didn't know how thick the ice was."

HERE, DURING THE ADVENT season, we hit the eggnog and the pecan fudge pretty hard, but if you want something good — and aren't on some cruel version of the Atkin's Diet — and tasty and healthy, especially if it is made with organic ingredients, then make this, or get someone to make it for you. You can eat this anytime in moderation. It makes a great Christmas gift for someone who has everything. Or nothing. It's from my friend, Mary Jane Clark who'd be glad to share it. Mary Jane isn't around anymore. She's either resting, all healed from her cancer, or possibly she's eating her granola and laughing with her first husband who left her via the windshield of a car one dark night when their children were small. In any case, I know nothing is dark for her now.

We used to eat this together in the morning, watching her cats stalk the butterflies in her garden in the foothills of Colorado's San Juan Mountains. I think if you make this and eat it, you'll feel better about most things. You'll definitely be more regular and there is both irony and joy in that.

Mary Jane's Granola

12 cups regular (thick-cut or long-cooking kind) oatmeal

1 cup of each of the following:

Sesame seeds

Oat bran

Powdered milk (optional)

Sunflower seeds

Nuts (pecans, cashews, whatever)

2 cups coconut

1 t. salt

2 t. cinnamon (optional)

Mix together in a large bowl.

In a small saucepan heat the following until the sugar is dissolved. Add to oatmeal mixture. Stir until well-coated.

1 T. vanilla

⅔ cup honey

⅔ cup brown sugar

⅔ cup olive oil

⅔ cup water

Place in 9x13 cake pans (makes 4 pans). Bake about 35 minutes at 350° until light brown and crisp, stirring several times. The recipe can easily be reduced. Before packaging in zip-lock bags add raisins, dried cranberries, or chopped apricots.

IRONY IS, AS ENGLISH majors know, "the incongruity between what actually happens and what might be expected to happen, especially when this disparity seems absurd or laughable." I especially enjoy irony in someone else's life, like Jeremy and the vomit. I'm not as keen on it in my own, but irony does happen. This is a story dedicated to the incongruity of God's mercy applied to who I am, which is irony of a sort.

In a large room decorated with construction cones, tool belts, and keychains with tiny replicas of hammers and screwdrivers as party favors, women sat around tables eating fabulous desserts, and, I supposed, contemplating the metaphor that surrounded them. "Extreme Makeovers" was the title for this women's event. Husbands and sons, awkward in the role of waiting tables, threaded between us with carafes of coffee and tea. I nervously waited to be introduced as the main speaker for this church's gathering of un-churched friends and neighbors.

Before I came to speak, Darcy, (not her real name) was on the program to give a kind of summary of what God has done in her life. Christians call it a "testimony." Darcy, a diminutive young woman with beautiful eyes, stood behind the podium and told us about her 15 lost years that began with a little bulimia and ended with her as a 68-pound anorexic and an abuser of alcohol and prescription drugs. Like addictions will do, they demanded everything from her, not only her body weight, but a few small items like her heart, liver, friends, family, and husband.

All she had left was this tiny, little shred of life when her younger brother came to tell her he, too, was finally giving up on her like everyone else. He told her, "You have ruined your life. You've ruined our family. When are you ever gonna change?" Assuming she wouldn't, he sat beside her crying for a long time and then left without hope. She'd been confronted many times, but something about her little brother's sadness completely broke her heart, and she marks that time as the turning point of her life. That night she threw everything down before God and cried out, "Help me. I need you. I want you."

That was two years ago and the beginning of Christ's remarkable redemption of her life. We sat at the same table together; I met her mother and her grandmother. Her husband was there too: he was out in the hall with their "miracle" baby in his arms — a round-faced, laughing little girl. He paced back and forth outside the auditorium praying for his wife. As Darcy got up, I saw her mom squeeze her hand and say, "You'll do fine." And she did. Darcy cried from the moment she began her talk until she ended with this passage from Jeremiah: "I know the plans I have for you, declares the Lord, plans to prosper you and not to harm you, plans to give you hope and a future" (Jer. 29: 11).

After this lovely story of amazing grace, it was my turn. It took about one second for me to realize that this was like the talented Emmylou Harris opening for an unknown, unheard of act. What I wanted to do was praise God, buy the CD, and go home. But I'd driven 250 miles to be there, and they'd also put me up in a very nice hotel suite with a nifty bedside radio and an ice maker *in the room!* I knew I had to face these women and begin with a confession about why I probably shouldn't even be there. Then they could go home if they wanted, since they'd already eaten their dessert and heard Darcy. The irony of this is that for a Christian my age, it would seem that the whole situation should have been, well, avoidable. So as they dabbed their eyes, I prepared to plunge ahead.

Last summer in the space of a few weeks, I received more invitations to speak than I had in the previous two years altogether. I was beginning to wonder if God was sending me a message. Like, you're an okay person even if you're a little discouraged and haven't cleaned the vegetable drawer in the refrigerator for six months. It's true that most of the invitations were not destinations, unless you've heard of Onalaska, WI, or Hinckley, MN. I just wasn't up to adding a speaking itinerary to my already anxious, over-wrought life. So I turned them all down except for this one, which I accepted quite by accident, though God may think otherwise.

I was having a weak moment just as I listened to the message my friend, Lisa, left on the answering machine about the possibility speaking at her church when the mail arrived with one of my favorite clothing catalogs — which I usually throw away. But this time, I said to my husband, as I leafed through, "If I find an outfit I like, I'll say yes." It'd been three years since I'd actually shopped for anything special. I won't mention which catalog because if I say it was K-Mart you might think I'm cheap and sleazy. But if I say Neiman Marcus, you'll wonder how I could afford them, which I can't.

I was stunned to find something I really liked. I even lapsed into Minnesotan, yelling, "Oh, fer cue-it!" Then I laughed, and looking at the ceiling, I announced, "I was only joking about accepting." Then I felt so wicked, I only hoped God had a sense of humor, so to be on the safe side, I decided I had to say yes to this invitation. You immediately see the problem: this wasn't because I cared about people or wanted to be used of God to encourage others.

The irony deepened when I learned the theme for the evening was "Extreme Makeover, Inside Edition," and how we are often tempted to live as if the most important thing is how we look on the outside. I should have just bailed. But I had already ordered that great-looking dress. Somehow, in my talk I managed to segue from the introductory confession into the idea that the central reality of our lives needs to be Jesus and that anything else we place there, even if it's a good thing, will eventually break our hearts. Which lately has been at the core of what I continue to learn about the Christian life.

Wherever Denis or I speak, we are usually invited to put out free samples of Ransom's publications and a sign-up sheet for our mailing list, which I did. At the end of the evening most of my samples were left, and of the 200 guests, only two people signed up for our mailing list. By human measures this event was a minus for our ministry. But, of course, you can never be certain what things God will do with the material he has to work with.

One good thing: I'm still here, and not so dull-witted that I can't appreciate the irony of my existence. It isn't divine oversight, as if God failed to notice what I was doing or saying. No, he sees me very well, and it is strictly a matter of God's loving kindness that I haven't been snuffed out.

The next day on the drive home I listened to one song in particular, not from a Christian group, as far as I know. Often, unaware, unbeknownst to the composer, a song can become a hymn that helps you find God in unusual places. I heartily sang Reindeer Section's "You Are My Joy" along with them. (from the CD *Son of Evil Reindeer*) The words are mostly a repetition of the title, which normally makes me think the songwriter was either in a trance or pressed the loop button too many times. But it works here as a lengthy meditation. I thought of my desire to make Jesus central to all my reality and that if he were with me, I'd dedicate the song to him, because after all I've eaten and drunk in this life he is still the best thing, my joy. Then, I thought, that if (if?!) he were with me, he might sing it to me. The notion of us being his joy is from Hebrews 12 which tells us he endured the cross for the "joy set before him." What he did not have before the cross was us. So I continued to sing, "You are my joy, you are my joy, you are my jo-oh-oh-wee" for both of us.

SCIENTISTS REPORT THAT CERTAIN species of bees kill giant invader wasps with body heat that comes within 5° C. of cooking themselves in the process. It was originally thought the wasp was stung to death by a ball of bees that surrounded it. But actually in what's called "heat balling" the bees raise the temperature by fanning their wings until the attacker dies.

Sometimes in life you don't know if you're the cooker or the one getting cooked. Either way, this year I've watched friends survive long enough to learn new meaning to the name Emmanuel, "God is with us." However adversity comes, God is certainly beside us, controlling the temp and getting heat-balled along with us. As he promises in Isaiah:

> When you pass through the waters, I will be with you; and when you pass through the rivers, they will not sweep over you. When you walk through the fire, you will not be burned; the flames will not set you ablaze. For I am the Lord, your God… you are precious and honored in my sight, and… I love you, I will give men in exchange for you.
>
> (Isa. 43:2–3)

There is no place for irony or cynicism in this. There is only surprise and joy that we could be so beloved. And so, we sincerely wish you a very merry Christmas and may you always be surprised by joy in unexpected places.

More Tremendous Trifles

MAY 1994

*I*N HIS WITTY LITTLE book *Tremendous Trifles*, G.K. Chesterton points out the weightiness of the small events, the little moments in our lives that define or change us. After twenty-five years of marriage, Denis and I are so familiar with our personal trifles, they are like old welcome mats greeting us at the front door. Often they require us to compromise and respect one another in new ways. During our first weeks of marriage, I was stunned by his habit of leaving dirty underwear on the floor. Really? After several days I kicked them under the bed. We "talked" about this, and it became an important small moment for me when he agreed to put them in the dirty clothes hamper from then on.

Denis enjoys a distinct ritual for tea-brewing. Pour boiling water into a mug with a *PG Tips* teabag, let it steep, remove bag, add a scant spoonful of raw sugar and a dash of whole milk. Simple. You'd think I could do this. At times when I have felt noble — like on his birthday, for example — I have made him a cup of tea in the morning.

Invariably, he would take a sip and pause; "This tastes odd. Did you rinse the teakettle before adding fresh water? Did you let the faucet run before filling it? Are you sure the water was *boiling*?" No. No, I did not. And yes — at least it was very hot. "What if from now on I make the tea and you make the toast?" Agreed.

We found, to our surprise, that in spite of years together some small new event emerges to enrich our relationship. There is an outstanding way in which Denis has delighted me the past few years. I pass it on because we have friends who are approaching the same point in their lives: Parenting kids in their teens.

When our children were young, I made most of the decisions about their lives: yes, you may run a lemonade stand at the park. No, you may not set up a telescope in our attic pretending to watch stars but in reality train it on our neighbors' windows. Yes, you may rearrange your room any way you like. No, you may not hop a train, ride it to the edge of town and skateboard back. (Years later, I learned he had done it anyway.)

As our children became teenagers, life grew more complicated. Decisions had to be made, not just about where to play and what to wear, but about bigger life issues. Such as: what time is curfew? Where am I allowed to hang out and with whom? Will good grades bring extra privileges? When do you get to drive the car? At 12:15 a.m. which parent goes out to pound on the hood of car when daughter rationalizes that sitting in driveway with boyfriend counts as being home on time?

Teenagers are lively, creative, and often filled with inappropriate humor (not that I didn't enjoy most of it), but they also try your patience because they are easily offended, always right, and constantly eating. During the middle years of family life, many of us find that careers become more demanding just as our children enter their teen years. As I watched Denis needing to spend more and more time with his work and less time with the family, I began to feel as if I was the only functioning parent.

This seemed to precipitate two problems: Our children suffered neglect from their father and he suffered neglect from me because I was busy trying to compensate for him. I had little time for our relationship. The more my life was devoted to our children, the more I ignored Denis and the more coldness and distance grew between us. We became more and more annoyed with one another. When he asked for some small thing from me, I had an excuse: *the kids*. When I asked him to spend time with the children, he had: *work*.

I can't give a formula for change. There just isn't one. It's easy for families to get stuck in a punishing cycle of demands and priorities. I know in our case, we both needed to shift our priorities. We needed to start by discussing the problem, but even talking about it was difficult because we were so defensive about our positions.

One day I read a familiar verse in Matthew's Gospel where Jesus asks, "Haven't you read… For this reason a man will leave his father and mother and be united to his wife, and the two will become one flesh? So they are no longer two but one. Therefore what God has joined together let not man separate" (Matt. 19:5).

This is how it usually sounds to me: blah, blah, blah, followed by a lengthy sermon on marriage and divorce. But this time it struck me that I was more one with my kids than my husband. I had definitely placed them first and for good reasons, I thought. If he wasn't going to spend time with them, then I must, mustn't I? Obviously, *one* parent is better than *none*. As I prayed about how right I was and how tiring it was to be me, it seemed like God was silent. So I tried another approach in prayer reminding God this was a temporary situation. *Just until they are older.* Then he could help me learn more about two becoming one. Still silence. Doggedly, I insisted that I had selflessly given everything to my children — including life, for pity sake — and now God was going to condemn me for that?

It was disturbing. I knew something was not right with my priorities. It wasn't all Denis' problem. Being deeply connected to him through marriage meant that our love and our time for one another should come first, before our children. It needed to be practical not theoretical. It was difficult to give up my justifications and when I did I felt anxious because I didn't know what would happen to our children. Perhaps they would feel unloved and abandoned by both of us. Perhaps Denis would make demands I couldn't meet. Perhaps neighbors would call social services to report that the poor Haack children were being neglected, and we'd never see them again.

Despite my fears, I began to consciously choose to give to Denis in some of what I considered to be trifling ways. Sometimes it was just a quick trip to Menards or help with a task. I even agreed to watch football games with him. At first, I didn't understand anything about it. It looked like giant apes ran together, tried to kill each other, fell in a heap, got up, did it again. With his patient explanations, I learned the game, enough to become a true, fair-weather Vikings Fan, loving them when they won and demanding they trade their quarterback when they lost.

I still don't profess to understand how this process works, but the interesting result was that over time, we changed a little. Denis became more active in fathering and I became more available to our relationship. He didn't need to compete with the children for my time as much anymore. Now the timing looks providential because I don't know how I would have managed the next few years without his help as a father.

IT COULD BE EASY to confuse being a good father with being a buddy to your children. But it isn't that. Fatherhood means being a loving, even sacrificial, leader and having the willingness to teach by example, not just words. As a child, when my siblings and I saw glaring inconsistencies in our dad's life and dared to mention them, he always boomed back at us: "don't do as I do, do as I say." That did not increase our respect for him.

Disciplining teenagers takes a lot of nerve and creativity. When Denis became more involved in our children's daily lives, the kids appreciated his fair, cool approach. One of my problems was that I responded to most requests with knee-jerk predictability: *no!* History had taught me that somehow, due to my children being basically cleverer than me, I could be drawn into countless arguments and complex maneuvers over the simplest issues. So I solved that by not listening. I just said "NO" to everything. Denis was almost disgusting in his ability to listen and remain objective. I admired how easily he stopped interminable cajoling and arguing.

Together we established guidelines and rules — if you don't have *some* rules what you get is a colony of rodents pillaging and running the household. But really, the fewer rules you have the better it is. We often had to remind ourselves that many things are not moral issues, although parents might be tempted think otherwise. (At one time, when we were childless and knew much more about childrearing, we imagined that most things were black and white.) Denis was good at hearing alternatives and making exceptions when appropriate.

Occasionally, one of them would approach me secretly planning to do an end run past a particular rule. They prey on my weaknesses knowing that if they argue with me long enough I'll grow tired of saying no and say yes even to shocking crimes. But now I smugly told them: "try asking your father *that* one." When that didn't work they tried humiliation. "What's the matter with you, can't you make a simple decision on your own anymore? Why do you have to hide behind Dad?" And other similar attacks on my self-image. (Kids should be given credit for being experts with natural skills for dismantling self-image.) But I have the answer to this, too: "fair is fair. For 14 years of your life I made all the decisions. Your dad is taking his turn now." It was a relief to have him as point man in this battle of wits.

WHEN DENIS BEGAN TAKING a more active role in fathering, it coincided with our son's decision to be done with me. It took a while to figure out what was happening. I know he couldn't have explained it either. I couldn't look at him without hearing a warning growl. Until then I had known almost everything there was to know about him. Who his friends were, what they played, what they said, what they thought, what girls they liked, what hurt, what made him happy, and who that was on the phone. We were so close we could finish each other's sentences when, suddenly, he called a halt to everything. He wanted nothing to do with his mother. I must not inquire about anything regarding his activities or his person. I must not say, "You're looking a little thin, you better make yourself a protein shake." I must not go into his room to investigate moldy smells. And I especially must not ask why he wasn't using that expensive cleanser I bought for his acne. I didn't know what I had done.

I finally understood this was a healthy stage of growth. Unless I wanted arrested development and a boy whose laundry I did every three days for the rest of his life, I needed to let him go. However much my heart was breaking, hadn't we planned for his independence from the moment he was born? It's easy to forget that by the time your child is a teen, your job is basically done. You've taught him what he needs to know and now he needs to decide for himself who he will be and who he will follow. Denis made it easier for me when I saw them on the porch late at night laughing and talking — about guns and women, I think. I've seen them read a Bible chapter together, bow their heads, then slap each other on the back on the way to bed. (I spy.)

When Denis first suggested they get together occasionally to read Scripture and pray before bed, he thought Jerem wouldn't be interested. Surprise! He was. Denis tried to keep it low key and informal. Those seem to be good times for them.

Things seem better between Jerem and I, but it has taken three years. He actually talks to me once in awhile even if it's only to take my hand, peer earnestly into my eyes and say in a voice meant to reassure a child: "Mom, I am going out with my friends now. Don't worry. I'll be home on time. Don't wait up for me. I am going to be okay."

It is remarkable how teenage children need their fathers, yet this may not be obvious until something that seems insignificant arises. This past year we were sharing with Sember, who is 16, some possible changes in our lives, such as Denis taking some courses at a university that might take him away for two days a week. It might mean not being home for dinner on those days. On hearing this she quit talking. With some prodding she finally put her head down and began to cry; "I don't want you gone at supper time."

Denis and I looked at each other in astonishment. This was our independent, self-assured daughter, the one who ignores us most of the time, the one who likes to go into her room and stay there for hours talking on the phone and listening to music — and when not in her room she is busy with friends and activities. The one who half the time isn't even home for dinner herself. We were shocked. Yet there it was, a "tremendous trifle" sitting right in front of us. She not only *needs* a father, she *wants* one. She looked up with a wan smile and said, "I may not be home, but I want *you* at home. Dad, you can't do this. And also, I thought I'd let you know, if we have to move, I'll probably commit suicide. Well, not really, I'm kidding, but you have to know it would be so hard for me that is what I would want to do."

All we were talking about was Denis being in a nearby city for two or three days a week. We can't necessarily tell from the surface how much our children need us to be there for them. Sometimes we don't find out until it seems too late.

On the day I met Brooke, the pain of her father's abandonment was not something that was apparent, nor could I have guessed it. We sat at the table drinking Pepsi, chatting about nothing. The thought that kept crossing my mind was how much God must love this wild-looking young woman, but I didn't know if I could. She was, she proudly informed me, half Italian and half Indian. She had beautiful dark eyes, a thick head of black hair, and at least one tattoo that wound round her wrist and up her arm. I wondered how to be open to her — to who she was; how to have a meaningful conversation with her and about *what*? I didn't have a clue. My eyes kept straying to her tattoo so I finally asked her what it was supposed to be. I didn't know my groping question would be the very thing to unleash a torrent.

It was a vine with flowers and a bee. She squeezed it and scowled. "It's so faded. The guy who did this was not a very good artist."

So how should it look? Don't tattoos fade after awhile anyway? "Oh, no. It should stay bright for the rest of my life. Like this one." And she pulled up her pant leg to show a detailed rose bush growing up her calf. "Or this." and she pulled down her shirt to reveal a unicorn dashing across her chest, its horn aimed for her heart.

The next question was one every non-tattooed person asks. Doesn't it HURT to get that done? "Not too much. I yelled a little for this one, but it was worth the pain because it is *so cool*." (The one across her sternum.) "Now this one I didn't even feel." She pointed to a cross on the web between her thumb and index finger. It was uneven and crude. "This made me so mad! I got hammered at a party, passed out, and woke up with a tattoo. Happens all the time."

I silently vowed never to pass out at a party.

Wow! was the not-very-profound response I came up with.

As though all the tattoo talk and been a warm-up for the deeper things in life, she began to reveal more: Her tummy was bumping out a little, and she confessed she was beginning to feel fat because she was going to have a baby. She was only 19, six months along and already divorced from the father. At a New Year's Eve party, he ditched her for a three-day drunk. When he came back she threw him out. She wasn't going to repeat her mother's mistakes, she said. For years her mother tried to live with an abusive man who destroyed their lives, until one day he left in an alcoholic rage and they never saw him again.

She had dropped out of school when she was 16 so she could party full-time. But now there was one good thing happening in her life, she had returned to school determined to finish and had just graduated from high school. When I asked what made her decide to go back she gave me a withering stare and said; "I grew a *mind*!" That week she was filling out financial aid forms for college.

Just then Jerem walked in to tell me his evening work schedule and say goodbye. I politely introduced him to Brooke, who watched our exchange. After he left, she swore passionately using f-words and exclaimed how handsome he was and how nice he was to me, and how that very quality was number one on her list for her next love: "He's gotta be nice to his mom, cause that's the way you can tell how he's gonna treat you."

After Brooke left, I felt a little dazed. The tattooed lady. She wasn't anything like I imagined when I first set eyes on her. She left an ache in my throat. She reminded me of all teenagers in a way. I wanted to mother her. I wanted her father not to have left his family. I wanted her husband not to have abandoned her at that party. I wanted her to know how much God loved her. And yet, despite her history and her suffering, she sat at my table confounding me with flashes of the image of God, although she gave no indication of belief. God had begun to smash my prejudices against people with tattoos.

For fathers who struggle to balance the parts of their lives to include parenting, for mothers who want their husbands to be significantly engaged in child-rearing, for single parents who need to be both Mom and Dad: in a way, a young woman like Brooke should give us great hope. She reminded me that, as Christians, we believe that every human being born into this world is stamped with the image of God. When it is revealed in unlikely places it can catch us entirely off guard. In a way it explains something about Brooke, growing up fatherless and now without a husband. Why is there creativity when everything ought to predict a lack of it? Why is there beauty when only ugliness seems possible? Why is there humor and hope in desperate situations? Why is there love when abandonment and broken promises are the only experience?

Because God has mercy on *all* his creation. Not just the good and the perfect. He gives certain blessings to all people regardless of whether they believe or not. Theologians call it common grace; thus Brooke with her beauty, her wit, and her seeds of common sense.

THE UNIQUE COMPLICATION FOR fathers that is associated with God's image is that they share the same name. God has chosen to reveal himself as Father; so we pray, "Our Father who art in heaven," for example. Human fathers, whether they want to or not, will influence their child's perception of what God must be like as a father. How can a child not draw comparisons? Between our biological father and our heavenly father? Both Denis and I had difficulties dissociating ourselves from the harmful legacies our fathers left. What they passed on seriously twisted our ideas about God's love, his mercy and what one must do to be accepted by him. This should compel us as fathers (and mothers, too) to place ourselves fully in God's hands, trusting that even in our failures he will guide us and forgive us and that nothing we can do will prevent God from caring for the hearts of our children in ways we never could.

There is another form of grace that should cause us joy: God's special grace poured out on those who believe because of Christ's great work in redeeming us. We all agree that we are each of us lost and in need of restoration, but as I see it, this is also the great Parent Leveling Factor. I like to keep this in mind, especially at church on Sunday mornings when some families look so perfect, so put together, while we look all rag-tag and reeling from a week of afflictions. No matter what façade we present to the world, we are not ever, ever going to be perfect parents. Not even if we attend every Sunday school class on parenting and read every expert's book on how to raise perfect children. Not even if we passionately pray, day and night, for help. We will make mistakes we regret. When we are tired, when we are stressed and impatient, when we have no idea what we are going to do with our wayward child and have even made matters worse with our own sin — God will be there in the midst of our sorrows and griefs. He pours special grace on those who believe.

We, who have become part of God's family not only have access to common grace, we receive his special grace that is poured out on us. I love how Paul phrases it in Ephesians. In talking about the incredible things we have in Christ, he says that it is all "in accordance with the riches of God's grace that he *lavished* on us with all wisdom and understanding" (1:8). The dictionary definition for *lavish* is to have someone spend *extravagantly* on you. It is to receive a *torrent* generously poured out! There is no quenching it. This is not specially directed to intact families or to people without problems. The only qualifier is to be God's child in Jesus, and when you are, that inevitably means he will continue to spend a whole lot of grace on you. It flows into all the trifles of life including the lives of our children and we parents who strive to walk with God down this challenging path. Comprehending just a fraction of this truth is, for me, a weighty thing. A tremendous trifle.

The Nutmeg of Consolation
CHRISTMAS 2011

I RECENTLY READ ABOUT A man who was sent to Indonesia with his family to live and work for a global corporation. He had a lively interest in natural history, so in addition to his regular employment, he began describing and drawing the island's plants. Having learned much about the flora from local people, he included extensive cultural lore and medicinal uses. He pressured himself to complete the drawings because he was losing his eyesight to glaucoma. The effort became a large body of work, so large that he hoped to get it published.

Then came a series of tragic events. His wife and daughter were killed in a tsunami. Shortly after this, his house burned down and all his drawings were lost in the fire. He eventually had them redrawn with the help of an assistant. He sent half of the manuscript back to Europe, but the ship carrying it sank. Finally, after 37 years of research, writing and re-writing, the completed manuscript reached his company's headquarters. However, the company decided to suppress publication declaring that the manuscript contained trade secrets having to do with medicines and spices.

The year it arrived in Europe was 1697. His employer was the Dutch East India Company. The author, Georgius Everhardus Rumphius, died in 1702 without seeing his work published. It was finally printed in 1741.

Rumphius' seven-volume masterpiece, *The Ambonese Herbal,* was not available in English until Dutch scholar E.M. Beekman began the enormous process of translating it in the year 2000. That same year he was diagnosed with multiple myeloma. He, too, pushed himself to complete this massive project. It was finished in November of 2008, just before he died. This past year, (2011) it was published post-humously by Yale Press. Beekman never saw his translation in print.

I wish I could have consoled both of these men, assuring them that in a few years their work would be noted and loved by many. They bring us knowledge, yes, but they also bring us the pleasure of knowing God's astonishing, elaborate works of plant-art on a tropical island.

THUS FAR, MY LIFE'S work and calling have not taken such a beating. Though I sometimes wonder about the meaning and worth of what I do. Or have done. I often feel small and insignificant. Perhaps I should have gone to law school or herded sheep. Sometimes I complain that all I do is grind coffee beans and update my status on Facebook.

I have a book that was not shipwrecked, but for years it went unpublished. I think of the hours, months, even years it took to write. The days of crabbiness and distraction my husband endured as I wrote. The many drafts, and the queries, and the rejections, and there it sat, its pages printed and bound on my shelf. I often wondered, "What was that other than a colossal waste of time and white paper?" (Unlike Rumphius or Beekman, I have lived, after all, to see

The Exact Place: a memoir published by Kalos Press in 2012.)

I'm not alone in desiring consolation and comfort for merely keeping on year after year. I've had many conversations with folks from all walks of life who have had vocational questions about meaning and worth.

A dear friend, who works in the top layer of a Fortune 500 company, has been a faithful employee, a consummate leader and team player for many years. Recently, she attended an event where a few were recognized for their good work and asked to tell their stories. She knew one of these rising stars well because she had trained him. As he spoke, she was at once happy for him and a little sad. I think we understand why. It wasn't her need for power or fame; it was the desire to be acknowledged, to know our work has meant something. The speaker ended his talk by saying, "I wouldn't be up here today without the help of a person who has made my success possible. She has been my mentor and model — someone who encouraged me when things were hard, but who was tough enough to make me grow a spine. I would like to thank her." Then, he said her name. It was as though God himself heard her heart and named her in front of everyone.

Consolation

LONG AGO IN THE same part of the world where Rumphius did his work, certain East Indonesian sultans were oddly referred to as *The Nutmeg of Consolation*. This may have been related to the value of nutmeg, which was once worth its weight in gold, and also thought to be a cure for the plague. It's an intriguing title. It has a spicy, comforting sound that makes you think of holding a pottery mug with both hands and lifting it to your lips — a soothing mix of apple-sweetness, wine and spice.

With the sultan, if you were lucky, you might find both the

pleasure of his rare presence and the power to remedy your troubles. You might be comforted, as his name implied. Might. If his curry agreed with him and his harem was in order. Of course, these rulers are dead now and their power is gone.

A similar title that has attracted my attention and deep gratefulness many times, appears in the Christmas story as told by Luke. It isn't noted often, yet the words speak comfort to a soul who considers them.

Two thousand years ago, Jesus was eight days old when he was brought to the temple for dedication and circumcision. Joseph and Mary weren't expecting a special welcome from the establishment, but for years an old, old guy had been watching for this very moment, and he spotted them in the crowd, a young couple carrying a baby just over a week old.

Simeon, we are told, was "waiting for *the Consolation of Israel*." (Luke 2:25) How long had he been watching for this person? How did he recognize this particular baby? Did the hair stand up on the back of his neck? The Holy Spirit must have blazed inside him, because hurrying over and taking God in his arms, he cried, "My eyes have seen your salvation, which you have prepared in the sight of all people, a light for revelation to the Gentiles and for glory to your people Israel."

The Consolation of Israel. An unusual title for a baby. John Calvin once wrote in a letter to a prisoner held in a French dungeon, and subsequently martyred, "We have wherewith to comfort ourselves in all our miseries, looking for that happy issue which is promised to us, that He will not only deliver us by His angels, but will Himself wipe away the tears from our eyes." Jesus is the only one with everlasting presence and divine power to console us from our sin. To comfort us in darkness. To allay the sorrow and the weariness of everyday life. To grant us worth and meaning, not only in our vocation and calling, but for our very selves.

Over and over, it is our privilege to offer up to Jesus the small, everyday works from our hands. It is the labor of my listening and writing. It is the apple puff pancakes I made this morning for house-guests. It is loving ten angora bunnies, tiny creatures of God, who dart to my feet expecting kale and carrots each morning as I step onto the back porch where they will live until our housemate sells them. Jesus is our comfort and consolation for things unfinished, for futures unknown. He is the keeper of life's collateral results hidden from our eyes.

The Consolation of Israel arrived with an express purpose: to re-store glory, one day, to everything that has gone awry. Peter refers to this in the book of Acts when he speaks of Jesus coming again. (Acts 3:19) This is part of the joy and comfort we share with Simeon as we wait for Jesus to finish what he has already begun.

A Note about *The Nutmeg of Consolation*

YOU MIGHT RECOGNIZE THIS as the title of a book in Patrick O'Brian's series of seafaring novels set in the early 1800s. In O'Brian's book it is both the name of a ship and a piece of music. In rare moments of peace, Captain Aubrey and Stephen Maturin, the ship's surgeon, played duets on the violin and cello. On one such occasion Aubrey asks Maturin, "I dare say, what was that last piece?"

Maturin's reply: "Nutmeg of Consolation."

Aubrey thinks about this and says, "That's it. Those were the very words hanging there in the back of my mind. What a glorious name for a tight, sweet, newly-coppered broad-buttock little ship — a solace to any man's heart... Dear Nutmeg. What joy."

Yes. To see the Nutmeg hove into sight, her sails sheeted to the wind, and you castaway on an island without hope of rescue? That, my friends, is Divine.

Parenting — I'm Done
MAY 1996

*T*HIS YEAR OUR YOUNGEST graduated from high school. This is a landmark for parents, like getting the last baby out of diapers. Sember is done with high school and it is a relief to have some kinds of parenting over. No more micromanaging sleeping and waking patterns (as if I ever succeeded). No more nagging about a junk-food caffeine diet. She can pierce her navel, throw a rod in her car, or live in Mozambique if she wants. We will sympathize and advise. But our primary work as parents is done and now I am going to sleep all night for the next 10 years.

After 26 years of parenting, you'd think I could claim to be an expert on childrearing and allow other parents to pay me for learning exactly how it's done. But it looks as if my only expertise may be noting the ironies and humor children bring to our lives. Running a close second is my remarkable ability to humiliate myself with failure and sin. I have learned to hope in the grace and power of God. I think.

The attitude we've tried to achieve through the years is beautifully summarized by Covenant Seminary professors Dan Doriani & Jack Collins in a little leaflet called *Rearing Covenant Children In Faith.* They emphasize "parenting in confidence without presumption." That is, "Confidence in the biblical promise that God loves and covenantally claims the children of believers." But, as they quickly add, this can be "misinterpreted as a guarantee that the children will be saved, if the parents carefully train them in the faith."

Doriani and Collins affirm two truths:

First, the children of believers differ from other children in that they have the privileges of covenant up-bringing. There is ground for confidence that the Lord sets them apart by placing his love on them. Second, we know that Adam literally raised Cain, that Isaac raised Esau, that David's favorite son betrayed him. (Each had the privileges of the Covenant but rejected the faith of their families.)… While warnings forbid overconfidence, promises instill a humble confidence in God's covenant provisions that inspires diligent obedience.

IN OUR EARLY YEARS we were plenty self-confident. We were certain that not only would we avoid all the mistakes our parents and friends had made, but that raising children was a snap if you just read the right books and paid attention to a few basic principles.

We had no idea what the grace of God delivered to us in the first bundle we brought home from the hospital. We loved her so much. She was the perfect baby. The perfect child — almost. We eventually discovered she had a few flaws, but overall, she was intelligent, sensitive, obedient, and compliant. We smugly believed we had shaped her ourselves. We were great parents, but probably anyone could do this if they just put their mind to it.

We had to wait six years for two more children whom God

especially designed with side benefits that could address our delusion and teach us a little humility. What a wonder they were! Delightful. Normal. Naughty children. However, they didn't fit into the nice little box I had prepared for them. It seemed that no matter what method I applied to raising these two, they tested my equilibrium in most areas of life. I couldn't seem to apply discipline with consistency. I lost patience. I couldn't seem to retain my old habits of prayer and Bible reading, which I thought were key to my spiritual and mental health. By just being children, their never-ending needs, their mischief and little rebellions, it didn't matter, day or night, they poked holes in my resolve to be a better mother. I was always starting over.

SELF-RIGHTEOUSNESS CAN PUT YOU at risk for a hard fall, so when I hit bottom my confidence in childrearing collapsed. I was hammered by at least two things: first, by the Experts who promised everything would be perfectly okay if I only followed their advice. The second hit was having to face my own poisonous nature, which I had somehow passed on to my sweet little munchkins. Almost every day they were a reminder of how unreasonable I could be.

I recall a day when a friend dropped off our order of fresh milk from the dairy. I was on the phone, so she set the two gallons of milk in glass jugs on the floor inside my front door. Only that morning I had told the children that when they had accidents — like spilling their drink at the table which happened every noon, like clockwork — that were not the result of disobedience; I would not be upset with them. They listened with big eyes to another of Mom's turning over a new leaf. Jerem was two and a half at the time, and when he spotted that milk he decided: "Me help, Mommy." With enormous effort he picked them up and staggered toward me. I turned in time to see him trip, clink the bottles together, and send a tidal wave of milk and glass across the entry and down the carpeted hall. I screamed and burst into tears, and then I spanked him.

We were caught in moments like this that shamed our hearts. We saw ourselves with new eyes. I imagined our children some day sitting in a therapist's office, weeping and saying, "My mother always..." or, "It was my father..." No matter how hard we tried not to, we hurt our children, usually unintentionally, but sometimes intentionally! On this side of heaven there wasn't a snowball's chance in hell for raising perfect children because their parents were so imperfect.

What confidence I had started out with was replaced with a boatload of guilt. I needed forgiveness from both God and our children.

IN THE MIDST OF learning we weren't such great parents after all, we really hoped the Experts would be able to help us calm down and smooth out the chaos of childrearing. It was unbelievable how many people claimed to know just what we needed. They had the exact solution (all of them different) for every problem your child or you might have.

The Christian marketplace is full of people who claim to have authoritative and comprehensive knowledge of godly parenting. They have devised techniques, steps-to-success, and principles for parenting. It's hard to miss these people if at any time in your life you've stepped into a Christian bookstore, attended Sunday school, or listened to Christian radio. As we sorted through the literature it became clear that both parents and the Experts often seized upon "one principle and stressed it to the neglect of other parts of biblical truth about parenting" (Doriani & Collins).

For example, one child-growth psychologist, popular when Sember was a baby, insisted that your child's entire psyché was formed by the time she was 18 months old, and that if you failed to love and stimulate her in the proper way — from *conception* — she would suffer failure for the rest of her life. That form of determinism stole what little hope I had, and I wondered whether I should just kill myself or give the kids up for adoption.

Dr. Dobson's *Dare To Discipline* was the parents' bible when our children were babies. He certainly helped us have the courage to discipline our children, but my mistake was thinking that his suggestions and principles were equally applicable to all children. So, for example, when I instituted his chart and reward system for doing chores I wasn't prepared for it to fail so miserably. It worked well for our oldest, who took responsibility seriously and wanted to please. But Jerem didn't have a shred of interest in stickers and stars. As for Sember, she was only mildly interested in the chart for its artistic possibilities and often stole the stickers and put them up in everyone's columns just for the beauty of it. We found that an "undue emphasis on methods can decline into self-serving attempts simply to control a child" (Doriani & Collins).

We tried seminars. We went to a five-day conference where we learned how to solve all our spiritual and family problems if only we would follow the steps of action presented to us. At the time it seemed so right and so possible. As days went by and predicted outcomes did not fall into place we were deeply discouraged. It was only in the following months that we began to understand the theological and practical problems with this approach. This was simply another form of determinism — the reducing of human behavior and relationships to a series of steps that, if you follow them exactly, are sure to trigger a divinely ordained outcome. This concept is not taught anywhere in Scripture.

Experts can be helpful, but their ideas must be thoughtfully examined. We should be cautious about listening to anyone who guarantees success or claims to have the final word on parenting. Legalism and self-righteousness is often a by-product of such books and programs. When young parents adopt the program an Expert recommends, they can be tempted to criticize other parents in their struggles or begin to moralize about why your child is having difficulties. It can also show up when parents seem to have especially compliant children who naturally respond well to the program. Not all children are made that way.

We live in a time when Americans have grown accustomed to quick fixes that can be applied to any problem in life. As Christians, we can't escape these pressures from our culture. Many have come to believe that complex relationships can be explained by simple principles. So if one discovers these principles and reduces them to a series of steps, one is assured of success. You can lose weight, invest finances, restore a broken marriage, and raise genius children if you faithfully apply their methods. Every few years when someone discovers the secret to successful parenting, we who deeply desire our children to love and obey God and succeed in this life, can find it tempting to believe claims that guarantee success, especially when the material is reinforced with Bible references discovered by the author.

However much we wish there were clear outcomes, Scripture does *not* give us step-by-step instructions for raising children with the complete assurance that they will enter adulthood as happy, healthy, productive believers — or anything else for that matter. We have a proverb (*not* a promise) that gives us hope that if we "raise a child in the way he should go when he is old he will not depart from it" (Prov. 22:6). Scripture provides some principles, and maturity and experience can supply some suggestions, but there is no God-authored manual with guarantees.

Notice the curious events surrounding Samson's birth (Judg. 13). His mother was barren when an angel came to tell her she was going to have a son, and that he was to be a Nazirite who would begin delivering Israel from the oppression of the Philistines. When she told her husband, Manoah, about this strange visitor, he prayed that God would send this person again *"to teach us how to bring up the boy who is to be born."* He must have been thinking of the awesome responsibility that had fallen on them. How they must have desired to do it exactly right!

The next time the angel showed up (theologians say there are reasons to believe this was the pre-incarnate Christ), Manoah asked him the big question. Will you "come again to teach us how to bring up the boy who is to be born?" What an opportunity this was for God to give us the final word on how to parent! I mean REALLY. If you were the Holy Spirit, how could you pass up the perfect chance to outline God's Way for Raising Children?

God's answer was basically, "Don't drink wine, don't eat unclean food, don't shave the boy's head, and do all I have commanded you." What?! This has nothing to do with character!

So the manual for raising successful children doesn't appear after all. Once again, God surprises us. What the angel told them was simply a repeat of what the Scriptures required concerning one who had taken the Nazirite vow.

THIS STORY MAY FREE me of my conflict with Experts, but I still had to deal with my failures as a parent. The only hope I found for forgiveness and a measure of healing is found in Jesus — in the way he has overwritten what I have done. Simply and beautifully put by Paul: *"He forgave us all our sins, having cancelled the written code that was against us ... he took it away, nailing it to the cross"* (Col. 2:13-14). That includes the ones that have hurt my children and destroyed my confidence as a parent.

Now I am allowed — and not just allowed, I am implored — to truly hope in God to be at work in my heart, in my family. Too often I imagine the power of God is available only for a spectacular crisis;

we don't get that it applies to ordinary situations, to the grind of daily life lived with our children. Paul describes this grace as God's *incomparably great power for us who believe. That power is like the working of his mighty strength, which he exerted in Christ when he raised him from the dead* (Eph. 1:19–20). God delights to enter into situations that are hopeless from a human perspective in order to perform restoration and resurrections of all kinds — but not necessarily according to our ways or timing.

When my confidence and mental health were somewhat restored, I could see I was not solely responsible for everything my child did. Ultimately, my heavenly Father was going to see about these things.

Again it is instructive to look at Samson's life. He is at once amazing and tragic. A child who grew up, and out of his parent's control. But never out of God's control. God used this very sinful and wonderful man, even in death. The account of his life in the book of Judges astounds me with its messiness. Betrayal, lies, revenge, violence, prostitutes, adultery, imprisonment and torture. If this were our son, it would not ever be the story we would want to live through, nor would we want to tell it to others. And yet in Hebrews 11 Samson is counted among those of great faith. Who can fathom God's ways?

AS A PARENT I also take courage from the story of Adam and Eve. God was their father. He placed them in a perfect environment. They had every opportunity to enjoy that privilege. God took such special care of them that he came every day to walk and talk with them in the garden. And yet, if *they*, in such a setting, choose to disobey God and plunge all of mankind into sin, isn't there the possibility that, despite my best efforts, my own dear children will make sinful choices? Sure.

My God is King. Savior. Lord. Redeemer. The father of Adam and Eve, the God of Samson. They aren't just meaningless names.

When he draws my children Home, they will be able to come to him despite my sin and failure.

So, having been forgiven, I want to raise my children by faith, as best as I am able, in the power God gives. In knowing him, I won't give up hope. I believe that according to his providence, all things are in his hands, including the lives of my children and the story is not over yet.

Comprehending a tiny fraction of this fills me with relief, and has sometimes allowed me to laugh at the ridiculous weight I placed on certain things. My mother raised six children and could tell us with authority that life wasn't as bad as we imagined and maybe we could lighten up a little.

This is what I'm talking about. Just for example. We live just beyond the one-mile boundary for our local high school, which according to their regulations, meant Sember was going to have to walk to school every day for three years; she could not legally ride the bus. Secretly, we grinned and rubbed our hands thinking what good discipline this would be for her. We thought *now* she will have to get up at a *decent* hour each day in order to make it to school on time. However, as everyone knows, walking takes a terrible toll on the lives of teenagers. Most of the time this could be avoided if only parents were thoughtful enough to buy them a car or drive them every day.

A few days after school started, we watched dumbfounded as Sember stepped out of a school bus that stopped in front of our house. In the mornings, one would pull up to the corner and patiently wait as she calmly descended the stairs in her stocking feet, toast in one hand, pausing on the porch to put on her shoes and, with the dignity of the Queen of England, stroll to the bus.

I was annoyed almost every morning. This was against the rules. Students were not allowed on a bus without a special picture ID issued by the district. I grilled her: "This is NOT a scheduled stop!

You DON'T have an ID. You should be walking! You could *at least* not keep that poor bus driver waiting for you."

Every year she patiently explained: "But the bus driver LIKES me and HE doesn't mind, so why should you?"

Every morning our neighbor across the street drank coffee on his porch, watched her and laughed at both of us. He said anyone that resourceful was going to go places in this world.

He was right to laugh. I finally gave up my insane campaign to make her walk to school. On the last day of October 1995, we snapped a picture of Sember regally entering the bus, had it made into a coffee mug, and gave it to our neighbor for Christmas with a thank you for helping us see a little more clearly and laugh a little more.

Psalms in the Dark

WINTER 2006

I'VE ALWAYS THOUGHT OF myself as intuitive because that is how I score on all personality tests. It is supposed to bless me with clarity of perception in the inner subconscious world, but it seems doubtful that I put that intuition to very good use. If I did, wouldn't I be perceptive enough to avoid useless tests of rationally constructed logic? Consider the following...

There is this growing popularity of Sudoku, the Japanese number puzzles, which at first I thought was just the fruit of poisonous minds — or at least ones without enough to do. Then they began appearing in our daily newspaper. After ignoring them for about seven months, I tried one and finished it in twelve minutes. I was so surprised and pleased with myself, I thought I might take that IQ test on mensa.org and find out if it cost anything to join them. The next night as I was relaxing in my chair with the sound track from *Grizzly Man* softly playing, and my husband quietly reading a seminary textbook, I tore out Tuesday's Sudoku and almost finished it before bedtime.

After supper on Wednesday I began my third Sudoku with a jaunty confidence. Two and a half hours later Denis begged me to please come to bed. I did, but I took it with me and worked on it for another hour without adding a single number. Only then did I notice five stars at the bottom of the puzzle with three of them shaded. A crack of light entered my darkened mind: Oh. This indicates difficulty factor. The one in my hand was a 3-star. The previous night's (with solution) was printed at the bottom; it had only been a 2-star. With logic gaining momentum despite intuition, it occurred to me that as the week goes by the puzzles increase in difficulty sort of like the NYT Crosswords so that by the time you get to the weekend they're so punishing you want to pay your own way to New York, find the editor, and force him to eat iceberg lettuce and Velveeta cheese until he can give you an eight-letter-word for "rugged outdoor clothing." Carhartt! Idiot! As *anyone* north of Minneapolis would know. And I don't want to hear, my friend, how you can do it in 10 minutes while blogging, writing a movie review, and flirting with the barista. By then I was crushed, in addition to feeling slightly crazy. But I rallied and told myself, "You've always despised logic, so why in the name of all your precious hormones don't you just intuit the solution? A few numbers should not defeat you."

Have you ever considered, even for one second, praying that God would help you finish a puzzle? Well. Okay. Maybe you haven't. But what about scoring a three-pointer from mid-court, or beating a red light? Or shooting a trophy buck? You know it's the same thing.

At 11:30 p.m. Denis raised an eyebrow at me and turned out the light on his side. I held the paper out for us to observe — it was covered with hundreds and hundreds of teeny, tiny numbers written in patterns, grids, and graphs. Suddenly, it was so scary because there it was: *A Beautiful Mind*! Remember that scene from the movie when the door of John Forbes Nash's office opens and on every wall, floor to ceiling, are little papers with hand-written numbers, formulas and codes, and you suddenly understood how ill he is, even though he is a genius? This was my mind on paper and it was not well. I shrieked, threw the paper and pen across the room, and turned off the light.

Calm Down

IN THE DARK I recalled a favorite Psalm:

My heart is not proud, O LORD, my eyes are not haughty;
I do not concern myself with great matters or things too wonderful for me.
But I have stilled and quieted my soul;
Like a weaned child with its mother,
Like a weaned child is my soul within me.
O Israel, put your hope in the LORD both now and forevermore.

(Ps. 131)

Of course, Sudoku is only a symptom — a metaphor of what's more generally wrong with me. As a mother I understand weaning a child. A baby has no idea why her mother made her stop doing her favorite thing in all the world. But in order to grow she must give it up. Her mother doesn't love her any less. She still encircles her arms about her baby and looks at her with shining eyes. Finally she quits her wriggling demand for milk and relaxes with her head on her mother's breast. Sometimes it takes weeks.

There's nothing wrong with solving Sudoku puzzles. It's just that for the most part, I can't. In a similar way, I often try to fix things too great for me. I push and strain trying to clean up the messes of life and am discouraged when I can't. Often I ask God exactly why he's not helping out a little here? But I am admonished by David to give up my demands. We must accept that if we minister and live in the real world there will always be certain matters in life that escape human solution — matters not resolved by efficient, practical minds or by sensitive insight either. I am redirected to quietness; to calming my soul. David turns away from inner conflict, and adjusts his focus outward: He addresses his people, "O, Israel." It's a place where we stand together in community, with the body of Christ, and we resolve to hope in the Lord forever and watch for glory to be revealed. We can never be certain of when or how God will appear as the One who is able to do "immeasurably more than all we ask or imagine" (Eph. 3:20).

The next day's paper had a 5-star Sudoku — the most difficult. I looked at it and calmly said, "I will not do this to myself ever again." And I put it in the trash. I think that's being weaned? Sometimes it takes years, but slowly I bend my head to God's shoulder and rest — even as I rejoice that Jessica, who is a bright, diligent L'Abri helper, says 3x3s are so easy she needs to do 4x4s to be challenged *in the slightest*. Then she adds, "Sudoku is something I can do without thinking at all, the answers are just obvious."

That is something far "too wonderful for me."

Falling House

LAST NIGHT DENIS TOLD me we need to save more money. Then he got a pained, far-away look in his eye like any minute he was going to excrete a kidney stone or something. It made me a little nervous. But when he said we needed to make some repairs on the house, I panicked. I'm usually the one who keeps a list of the parts of our house looking slummy and downtrodden. Like the stairwell, which fortunately, I can now ignore because it's so high I've been able to train myself not to look up at the plaster dangling off the ceiling in large flakes — or worry about them lacerating my skull if they fall when the front door slams. As long as the dishwasher is loaded properly and I don't leave too many blankets flung about the living room, Denis is fairly content to ignore the house; it suits me fine that he leaves the painting and repairs to me. So I held my breath and tried to imagine what was so bad he wanted to save money for it. I tried to keep my voice level.

"So what repairs did you have in mind?" I was hoping it was just the bathroom window, which we already agreed needs to be replaced because it no longer rolls in tight against the frame. When it was stuck a couple of summers ago, I stripped the threads of the handle by gripping it with both hands and cranking as hard as I could. Now you can see a tiny strip of skylight all around it if you look closely at the edge. And worse, you can feel cold air pour into the shower when you stand there in the morning waiting for that blast of hot water to save you. Anyway, that window is old and warped — it's one of those Anderson awning windows so it can't be completely my fault. (We should buy Marvin Windows, not just out of loyalty to our son, Jerem, who works for Marvin's, but because they make the very best windows in the whole world. However, they cost that much, too.) We had a man from Larson's Windows out for an estimate last week. He's so good at what he does. Just stood in our bathtub, whipped out his measurer, squinted his eye and said $850. Just like that. When we hesitated over triple thermal-pane glass he said, okay, a hundred dollars less, but you won't want to go cheaper than that. Er, I guess a guy could save a little more with a slider instead of a roll-out.

It wasn't the window that was bothering Denis after all. He told me, sotto voce, that before the L'Abri conference in mid-February, he'd gone up to the attic where we store boxes of his out-of-print book, *The Rest of Success*. A number of years ago the publisher let us buy up remainders for very cheap. I don't mean to get sidetracked. But do you see the irony of that? *"The Rest of Success: What the world didn't tell you about having it all?"* Still, we're so lucky to have this big attic that is the third floor of our house and can hold so much stuff it's going to kill our kids when we die because they're going to have to stand up there wondering why I saved those lamp shades. *BECAUSE*, I'll tell you now: they're antique 1930s Flapper-girl bedroom lamp shades, and could be worth a lot of money. But probably not enough to repair the roof.

Anyway, up in the attic Denis noticed that two full boxes of books are completely soaked with water. WHAT?! I wanted to scream. For many thousands, we just had our roof REPLACED five years ago! I needed to breathe into a paper bag.

Denis tried to calm me down: it's winter. No rain right now. We'll wait and I'll go up there and try to see where it's coming in the next time it rains.

Are you kidding? This is Minnesota! Due to global warming, have you not noticed the two inches of rain we got in early January? Or the snow that's fallen and melted about 20 times this winter instead of remaining on the ground until Memorial Day?

In bed that night I stared at the ceiling. *The Rest of Success* boxes are sitting right above us. I can't stand this breach in the very roof over our heads. It's like being told you have a mushroom growing out of your foot and the doctors will keep an eye on it until it begins giving off spores and shows signs of spreading up your calf, then they'll see if they can remove it. Of course, by then it will be too late and you will die.

I thought of the things we think we need: New shoes because, speaking of feet, my heel is hurting, which, when I Googled, Dr. Footdoctor said was plantar faciitis; oh great. A new car because how long can our 10-year-old Taurus keep driving across country? I can keep on sitting in a seat that is so custom molded to my rear, it has sunk to the floorboards. I can keep on slamming the glove box shut. So what if it spontaneously falls open on my knees about five times a mile? It's not much to ask when the roof needs fixing.

Songs of Joy

FOR SOME MYSTERIOUS REASON the psalm that scrolled across the ceiling that night was both comforting and beautiful.

Blessed are those you choose and bring near to live in your courts!
We are filled with the good things of your house, of your holy temple.
You answer us with awesome deeds of righteousness, O God our Savior,
The hope of all the ends of the earth and of the farthest seas,
Who formed the mountains by your power, having armed yourself with
strength,
Who stilled the roaring of the seas, the roaring of their waves, and the
turmoil of the nations.
Those living far away fear your wonders;
Where morning dawns and evening fades you call forth songs of joy.

(Ps. 65)

By his Word and his unfailing provision year after year, I am utterly convinced of God's care for his people and of our ultimate destination. But I feel convicted by lack of joy. There is a Haiku poetry feeling to part of the psalm — a powerful simplicity that condenses and intensifies the presence of God everywhere on earth.

Where morning dawns
And evening fades
You call forth songs
Of joy.

Farther than my eye can see, horizon to horizon, if we listen, we can hear God, coaxing us, inviting us to sing. Sufjan Stevens is one who hears songs of joy. (Sufjan's brilliant, creative music defies categories and is not found on the Praise Music scene.) He completely redeems, what for me was an — I'm sorry — annoying old hymn. With banjo and simple vocals, so quiet, so profound, he sings "Come Thou Fount." I didn't mean to cry, to be taken by joy with a hymn I knew so well and formerly resented from my childhood. Every word of every

147

verse came back unbidden.

> Come thou fount of every blessing, tune my heart to sing thy grace.
> Streams of mercy never ceasing call for songs of loudest praise.
> Teach me some melodious sonnet sung by flaming tongues above.
> Praise the mount I'm fixed upon it. Mount of thy unchanging love." (Verse 1.)*

It's not as though Psalm 65 or "Come Thou Fount" repairs our roof or heals my friend's body which is being hijacked by cancer. I know that. It is meant to give sorely needed hope and perspective. It invites us to look beyond the confines of our own lives and be assured that, even if it's the end of a particular chapter of life, it is simply not the end of the story. Now and then we catch glimmers of another dimension all around us — a stream in the desert, a child snatched from danger, a song of joy. Sometimes in small ordinary ways we experience the presence of God, as in the ability to get out of bed in the morning and keep our children alive. Other times we know for certain in the way a particular thing has fallen out, by its timing and our lack of control over it, that a we've witnessed an unusual gift of grace. A miracle really, though we hesitate to call it that.

A Postscript on Joy

IN HER BOOK *JULIE & Julia*, author Julie Powell writes about how she decides to make ALL 524 recipes in Julia Child's *Mastering the Art of French Cooking* in one year and blog about it. I persevered to the end of the book to find this incredible acknowledgement on the last page from someone who is at once talented, profane, and pretty far from God (possibly).

Julia taught me what it takes to find your way in the world.

---

* Sufjan's version was released in his Christmas album.

It's not what I thought it was all about — I don't know, confidence or will or luck. Those are all some good things to have, no question. But there's something else, something that these things grow out of.

It's joy.

I know, I know — it's truly an obnoxious word, isn't it? Even typing it makes me cringe. I think of either Christmas cards or sixty-something New Agey women in floppy purple hats. And yet it's the best word I can think of for the heady, nearly violent satisfaction to be found in the text of Julia's first book. I read her instructions for making béchamel sauce, and what comes throbbing through is that here is a woman who has found her way.

...I didn't understand for a long time, but what attracted me to MtAoFC was the deeply buried aroma of hope and discovery of fulfillment in it. I thought I was using the Book to learn to cook French food, but really I was learning to sniff out the secret doors of possibility.

Julie Powell precisely identifies our postmodern fear of joy. We're just cynical enough to think exhibitions of happiness will make us seem simple-minded, unsophisticated. And if we can't be rich or sexy we sure hope we can be profound.

So I'm none of these things. But as it happens, I can cook, and oddly enough, it seems to be one of my songs of joy — except that I believe joy is given by God and poured out as common grace upon humankind. Which means, give me an oven and I can slow-cook a chunk of moldy bread and make it smell so good Denis wants to eat in the middle of the afternoon. Yesterday I made a recipe of German beef short-ribs which I found on allrecipes.com. (I actually do use the web for more than fanning the flames of my mental illnesses.) I started them early in the day because I thought the last stage would require hours of baking in a Dutch oven. But they were done in only about three hours, and Denis was driving me crazy trying to eat them before supper. I totally refused him because I planned to make mashed potatoes and sauerkraut to go with them. *Gloria Dei.*

A Gentle Madness
WINTER 2014

"**P**EOPLE HAVE ALWAYS COLLECTED things. Whether a vestige of our hunter-gatherer days, a need to forge order amid chaos, or a simple desire to have and to hold, the urge to possess is a hallmark of the human psyche. Yet pathology is a danger. Compulsive hoarders find value in everything. Others fixate on a single thing, succumbing to what author Nicholas Basbanes calls 'a gentle madness.' In 1869 the bibliophile Sir Thomas Phillipps said he needed 'to have a copy of every book in the world.' His final tally (50,000 books, perhaps 100,000 manuscripts) wasn't bad."

("The Things They Brought Back," *National Geographic*, 1/14)

AS WE PREPARE FOR a move that we pray happens later this year, we are looking into closets, corners and other hidey-holes in the house. What to sell, pitch, or move? Denis and I each have collections we think indicate pathology or at least a "gentle madness" in the other. He has too many books, and I have too many containers of unidentifiable organic stuffs in the refrigerator. He accuses me of housing colonies of cholera — little does he know that that gelatinous mass of kombucha tea could improve his health, if only he would drink it.

But, I ask, shouldn't some of his books go away, especially titles which no one, not even he, will crack again? We have 23 bookcases packed full! At one point he reluctantly agreed to get rid of most of them. I know it hurt because they are his friends, but he had steeled himself. When our Board of Directors learned about this plan, one (who won't be named), in the time it takes to wave a hand, dismissed the idea, saying Denis should keep them! Otherwise, how would he do research? Several others agreed. Check. Mate. Perhaps they will help us move.

Still, I don't think 7,000 books compare to the refrigerator Denis frequently visits trying to sneak things into the trash without my knowing. Things I am saving. Like creamy horseradish sauce, pepperoncini, capers, fish sauce, Angustora bitters (What are they for, *anyway?*)… all these necessary ingredients for that wonderful something I might make some day. When I catch him with his head in a shelf crying, "WHAT'S this??? You never use it! It looks like rotten raccoon carcass! I'm throwing it out!" NOOOOO. That's like me throwing away all the obscure titles Francis Schaeffer wrote over the years. No. Do not throw away my fermented carrot condiment which I made and which I may or may not begin eating everyday for the microbial health of my intestines.

LITTLE BY LITTLE, WE have begun to sift through 33 years of home-making at Toad Hall. Today, in early January, I'm going through my filing cabinet. Back, back into the dark ages of my life. Dumping, dumping. Throwing files of essays, clippings, reviews. Children's authors. Crocheted blanket patterns. Homosexuality. Bank loans. Pathetic poems by Margie. Trying not to stop and read and wonder: WHAT was

I thinking? It is easier to de-clutter and pitch when I remember that I'm lightening the load my children will one day bear to the trash. It will be one less box to handle when I die. I don't think my death is immanent, but I'm motivated.

It's more difficult to know what to do with jewelry boxes that belonged to Denis' Aunt B and Aunt Ruth. Fake pearls, pop-beads, paste diamonds, heavy bracelets. Strangely configured brooches. Nothing of much value. Is there a granddaughter who would love these things? Perhaps turn them into glittering sculptures? Add them to vintage clothing? I don't know.

So, through the house I go, from the attic to the basement sorting, deciding. A few items sold on Craig's List, others posted "Free", some taken to Salvation Army. I know this purging is doing me good because when the single bedspreads and button collections are gone, I feel freer, lighter.

We laugh about these things, but underneath I am anxious. How we will manage the future? Why does every little thing need to be a hurdle of spiritual growth for me? It seems as if I am constantly being prodded to reach a level of maturity I can't achieve — that elusive place where I finally trust fully in God's interest in all my un-historic struggles. I constantly stray.

Take the Tour

If things go as planned by early March we will be ready for the 360-degree "show-off the home" show with bare surfaces, artfully placed bowls of fresh fruit, as if no human has ever put their feet on a coffee table. Our house will never look better, but don't you dare believe we live like that every day. When we are finally listed — watch our Facebook pages for the MLS listing and you might be able to visit us at Toad Hall for the last time. I know that over the years many of you have wished you could stop in. We do, too. I would have had everyone of you, if it were possible.

Two weeks later

WE ARE BACK FROM our annual Board Meeting which was in Chicago this year at Donald and Mary Guthrie's. Our directors are all old friends, peers who know and love us well. We've all been through much together. Their role in our ministry and lives seems to involve three things in varying degrees: Directing. Consulting. Blessing. We trust them.

In our discussions this year as Denis and I outlined what we think of as the next phase of life — a gradual reduction of some responsibilities over a period of years, a move to a home on one level, and a look at what increased writing might involve — the Board sharpened their focus and tackled: *where?* We had been looking in an area north of Minneapolis and St. Paul. A rural area where we might own several acres and to tell the truth? It is sort of in the middle of nowhere. The questions they piled on boiled down to: *what* and *who* are you moving to?

Well, we're moving to Margie's dream: to expansive horizons with birds and wild animals. To gardens and no traffic or helicopters. To quiet beauty. (Denis was with me in this, but easier to please.)

I don't know how it happened that I determined we should move to "nowhere farm," because we have often advised people about *where* to move when they faced a big change. We say you must not move without considering *where* and *who* your community will be. What church or body of Christians will you become a part of? Who are the people who will be your friends? Everyone ought to have people with whom you develop deeper relationships — more than just a friendly wave at the checkout counter or a "peace be with you" at the appointed hour in church.

Processing

As I WRITE THIS, we are still processing and I'm trying to understand how I could have blown past all our own advice. In her book *Another Country*, Mary Pipher warns people our age not to move to some exotic location where you've always dreamed of living but then in the following few years as your health disintegrates you are far away from a community of friends and family who would surround you with help when you are deeply in need (that phrase scares me; I don't WANT to be in deep need). Community trumps location in Pipher's mind. I didn't think I was ignoring her advice. It's not like it was the Florida Keys or Flathead County, Montana. But in fact it is pretty dreamy, when I'm forced to think of it. Imagine me being 76 (in ten years!). It's 30 below. The porch is sheeted in ice. The car won't start. Denis is sick. And we live 45 miles from the ER in St. Paul.

Then there is the *Anita-Factor*. She's been with us for almost six years now as our assistant, and her work has been incalculable. She has owned many things; she doesn't just complete a list of duties, but rather she comes alongside with her own initiative and gifts. But lately, she, too, has sensed a need for change. We love one another, so that isn't the reason for wanting new direction. She and I share a lot of likes, and I fantasized breathing fresh air while she did the chores, raised chickens, and mended fences. Yes, I imagined her still doing all her Ransom work, too. It's embarrassing to admit I willfully ignored her signals about needing change, *and* the Board's suggestions that when we move, we *need* to look for a place where we could live minus what Anita can do, because in the near future she may need to find a different position for many good reasons.

As for what's to become of my dream? I am emotional about it. And confused — feeling one thing now and the opposite the next day. On one level, I am quick to accommodate. That's what I did at our Board meeting when pressed about where we should live. I immediately saw my inconsistency. Then, as the people-pleaser I am, I quickly gave up my dream to saying, yeah, I could live here with a narrow little view in a Chicago suburb. So fine. Give me a row house with a microchip yard.

On another level, I'm angry with God. Why doesn't he just give me what I want with a lot less fuss? I've worked hard all my life. I deserve this little piece of cake. I also embarrass myself because I almost always process things verbally. So after blabbing, (like I'm doing here) everyone knows what I'm thinking. When I'm forced to change my mind, I have to go back and say, "oh, sorry, that's not going to happen." Not even close. So, here I am acknowledging that a place in the country won't be likely.

As often as I return to these wise words, they remind me of God's love:

> God knew the worst about us before he chose to love us, and therefore no discovery now can disillusion him about us in the way that we are so often disillusioned about ourselves, and quench his determination to bless us. He took knowledge of us in love.

> (J.I. Packer)

Revisions

WE HAVE LIVED THROUGH many crises and changes and seen how faithfully God delivers us time after time, year after year in ways I couldn't have imagined. But I still can't confidently shout: Don't worry about where you will live or... "what you will wear..." Or as the Message puts it: "Don't fuss about what's on the table at mealtimes or if the clothes in your closet are in fashion. There is far more to your inner life than the food you put in your stomach, more to your outer appearance than the clothes you hang on your body. Look at the ravens, free and unfettered, not tied down to a job description, carefree in the care of God. And you count far more." (Luke 12:24)

I know it. I know it. I know it. But, God help me, I still doubt. I don't know where Home is!

A prayer from *Common Prayer* touched my cloudy eyes today:

Lord, we all suffer varying degrees of blindness. We are blind to love, to justice, to grace and to life. Help us not to condemn one another in our blindness, but rather to work together to help one another see more clearly by your light.

(*Common Prayer*, January 22 by Clairborn, et al)

I am so happy not to be condemned by others (like by our Board) for my blindness. I'd even be happy if I learned not to condemn myself for blindness.

People don't normally write about things such as this to their mailing list — although many of you are personal friends. It seems, well, UN-spiritual in the way of ministry newsletters. However, declaring it "un-spiritual" is antithetical to all we've stood for over the years. We maintain that there is not one square inch of life over which Christ does not reign. So all this dilemma and fogginess is part of our being human, struggling with our own faultiness and finiteness. It is exactly what God wants to take us through right now, even though I hate the uncertainty.

In some corner of my heart, I can give my hopes and dreams to God for safe keeping. I don't know where we will be in six months. I know there could be a spot for us that is more urban yet doesn't rule out a clear horizon and a quiet neighborhood. And if not? Will I eventually find grace and contentment in where we land? I think so.

I'm going to watch to see how all this turns out. In the meantime, if any of you understand just a portion of this — if you have lived counting down the days to some inevitable change in your life, then

I'm comforted. You can pray for us. You are my friend.

Lord, to laugh in the midst of trial and to rejoice in the darkest valley is another way of saying. 'Our hope is in you.' Fill us with laughter and joy while we work for peace and strive for justice. Amen.

(*Common Prayer,* January 27)

The Mountain Ash

SPRING 2013

THIS PAST SUMMER WE lost our mountain ash. For three years it has shown signs of sickness. The first year I was hopeful. It was just my imagination. It was a dry year. Leaves were withering and falling in mid-summer. When I looked closely at the bark, in places it looked like it was giving up the trunk, loosening like a roll of paper towels ready to unravel.

The next year I noticed dozens of small, even holes drilled in such perfectly straight rows you'd have thought a tiny engineer with a miniature drill was at work, but it was woodpeckers going after wormy invaders. Normally, the tree produced clusters of bright red berries each fall but last year they, too, were sickly looking. The crowds of cedar waxwings that visited once a winter to feast on them did not come. In hopes of stopping the spread, we cut off the worst-looking limbs. The continued yellowing of branches at the ends of main limbs sent me googling on arborist sites. It was useless, like chemotherapy for stage IV pancreatic cancer. It had fire blight, an incurable bacterial infection.

Sadly, we cut it down. The cross section of the trunk showed dark streaks, evidence of the secret disease that ran up its vascular system plugging its only way to get nutrition.

Mountain ash is a northern tree that likes cold winters. I planted this tree 10 years ago in memory of my Frolander Grandparents. Mountain ash thrived on the resort Grandpa and Grandma owned on a remote island on the Canadian side of Lake of the Woods and at their winter home in the town of Warroad, Minnesota. Mountain ash don't need rich soil, they efficiently pull nutrients from rocky, cold earth. They often grow up clump-like, as birch do, sending up several strong leaders from the ground that eventually become trunks. Their branches bend in graceful arcs especially in fall when berry clusters weigh them down. However, the farther south they roam, the more susceptible they are to fire blight. So Rochester is a trial for them.

This past fall, as we often do, we headed to the North Shore of Lake Superior where a friend owns a cabin about 50 feet from the water's edge. Here is where we've been fortunate enough to land for a restorative week now and then. The south-facing windows give a full view of cold, rocky shoreline and glorious sunrises and sunsets. One week here can make up for months of city-living bounded on all sides by neighbors and trees. All along Highway 61 we passed mountain ash glowing wildly, bent with scarlet berries. They shone among forests of yellow birch leaves, white trunks and dark evergreens.

More of This, Less of That

MOUNTAIN ASH TREES POIGNANTLY remind me of my Grandpa and Grandma who loved me well as a child. Now, it is odd to think that I am a grandparent yet I still miss them. I've reached their time of life. We have eight grandchildren, and beyond wanting to love them well, we are becoming more familiar with the changes and limitations this age brings. Here we are, Denis and I, just passing 65 and entering this inevitable stage of life that everyone slides toward. We aren't ready to retire yet, but we are actively considering the changes knocking on our door.

The auto-immune issues I live with can sap my energy and fog my brain. There are days when lifting the lid on my computer eludes me. I cancelled my October trip to Alaska for a women's retreat because at the time, I didn't think I could manage it. More often now I hear Denis say, "Let's just have a quiet evening at home, please?" I can't do hospitality at the same pace as I used to and everything else about Toad Hall that we've loved doing for years. Not anymore. We couldn't have done the past five years without help from Anita, our assistant. I've wondered, apart from the physical, why can't I accomplish more here? I think I know. God seems to be leading us in a little different direction. We've concluded we need to leave Toad Hall.

In a NPR interview, the music duo *Over the Rhine* recently talked about their latest CD and some things that resonated deeply with my heart: Karin Bergquist said, "We lived in the city for a long time and we loved it. It just became more and more obvious to us that we needed a change when we would get home from tour, traveling city to city; we started craving something else. And so, this last chapter, the last eight years of our lives, have been centered around this farm. [*Nowhere* Farm in Ohio.] It's about an hour outside of the city. I wanted coffee and birds and dogs and silence; I just needed that for a change.

"There's a line in there [from a song titled "Meet me at the Edge of the World"] about how we're standing on this cold concrete, we're performing on this stage and we're so, so grateful for the audience that is here — but there's still that calling, that craving to be alone and to be someplace where we can sort of collect ourselves and plug in and rejuvenate and recover. That's where the songs come from, that moment of recovery."

I don't think of my life as being on a stage where I perform or pretend to love a life filled with people and all sorts of urban things. I have loved it for all these years. But for 32 years it has been something of a public life. Now, it seems that rather than just being off for a few weeks during the year, I need a more permanent place where quietness and rejuvenation happens almost daily and allows us to write not songs, but words.

Somewhere Near the Edge with a View

ALL MY LIFE I have longed for a more rural setting, but heeding God's call has meant living in the city. So we created a place of shelter and discussion and hospitality and writing. We made a small garden in the midst of sirens and helicopters from St. Mary's, garbage trucks, and buses that course by Toad Hall.

That farm I grew up on had its difficulties, but its long horizons and starry nights have never left me. It still calls to me in a way I hardly recognized or owned as a younger woman. I've always said to Denis that, when I am old, all I want is a "Room with a View." Remember that movie? Of course, I've amended that a little. Now I add: hardwood floors, a burr coffee grinder, a comfy bed on the main level because some days I haul myself up the stairs like an old goat with a cane.

A country setting is not where we plan to do NOTHING, but more a place where as long as our battered brains hold up we will write and include some thoughtfully chosen travel gigs. Lots of folks have asked if there would be a next volume of *The Exact Place*. It's somewhere in my head, but I need to get there fast as memoires flee from me. My editor would like me to (kindly) get off my duff and pull together a collection of *Notes*.

My heart longs for the horizon — a place where my eyes rest

somewhere beyond my desk, where I sit with a Mac and a cup of coffee — looking at that distant place where the sun rises and sets. I'd like to see a field with wooly animals, fainting goats, and a little coop with five or six barred hens. I'm sure those creatures will help me remember who I am and what God made me for. Perhaps then the refreshment I seek will turn into fruit that God might be pleased to use in my final run down to the end of the garden.

So, this is, perhaps, the winter of our lives. Or at least late fall. There is still lots to be done. I'd like to keep going with *Notes From Toad Hall*. Denis wants to keep writing *Critique*. I'd like to keep on letting you know how this aging bit goes. Is it possible to serve God well with failing body parts, Social Security and Medicare? We plan to lean into this and listen and learn new ways of being faithful in the midst of our ordinary. We'd like to be signposts of encouragement to others. We are going to avoid the advertisements of our culture that insist "You can do ANYthing you want no matter how OLD you are." Bah. Denis jokes that we're not quite ready for assisted care, but with a play on words, says, "perhaps we will name our next home "The Out House," referring to the last place we will own somewhere out there on the prairie on our way out of life. And, Bonus! he suggests I write "Sheets from the Outhouse." Maybe. Maybe.

Say 'I Love You'

Christmas 2012

When I grew up and moved away I rarely saw them. But in December of every year I especially remember my grandparents. Each December I carefully add a small collection of bubble lights to the tree, carefully placing them just so because, I admit, too many would be slightly cheesy. Their gentle movement and glow add a dimension to our Christmas tree that I must have — the memory of my grandparents' tree in full regalia.

Grandpa and Grandma Frolander made Christmas special for our family of eight. And, just as importantly, they never forgot my birthday, which was December 15th — a birth date easily rolled into Christmas. Some years on Christmas Eve they drove drifted country roads far out to our small farmhouse bringing two (two!) presents for every child. Grandma also brought tins filled with cookies. Tender thumbprint cookies with a dollop of apricot jam in the center, fragile Swedish rosettes dusted with powdered sugar, pressed butter-cookies in the shape of bells decorated with tiny silver balls. Every thing she did was precise and beautiful.

Sometimes I went home with them and in the morning when I awoke in a chilly bedroom alone, I would creep down the stairs and climb into my grandparents' bed. Grandma would already be up making breakfast — the coffee pot wheezing in the kitchen, the air filled with the scent of bacon. Grandpa would be in bed still listening to NBC News on the radio. I would snuggle under the blankets and he would reach over, just as I knew he would, to pinch me. I would scream. He would tickle me. I would hit and kick him. He would grab my fingers and not let go until more screaming and laughing. It was a good way to begin Christmas vacation.

Say It. Say, 'I Love You'

WE WROTE SOME OVER the years and twice they visited us in New Mexico where Denis and I lived for 12 years. The last time Grandma remembered my birthday was December 1980. A few days after she mailed the card, they both died. Grandpa had finished lunch that day and moved to his living room chair where he was finishing the wooden clocks he had made for his grandchildren. They were gathered around his feet ready for clockworks and hands. After Grandma washed the lunch dishes she went into the living room to knit and found him sitting unnaturally still, his head fallen forward. She called my mother, who lived 36 miles away, to say, "Dad has just died."

Mom told Grandma to hang on, and she would be there as fast as ever she could. When she arrived in Warroad she saw the ambulance in their driveway and a crew carrying a body out of the house on a stretcher. She assumed it was her dad and did not, could not, comprehend the shocking words that, no, this is your mother. She has gone, too.

As the family gathered from far away places, Mom and her brothers met at the house to plan, to be together. I listened to their talk and tried to grasp, tried to believe that both Grandpa and Grandma were gone. The house was decorated. Sitting at the kitchen table drinking Grandma's coffee and seeing plates of Grandma's Christmas cookies, divinity and fudge on the counter, I remembered the loveliness of her hands as she baked and carefully decorated dozens of goodies. Now this surreal moment as we sat nibbling her sweets. How could she not be here?

I regretted that I hadn't thanked them enough for their gifts, for their love. So my advice is: say it. If your grandparents are living say: I love you. Say it now. I only wish that I had taken more time to write and call. I believe I will see Grandma again, and will be able to tell her how much I love her. We aren't as certain of Grandpa, but there is evidence that in his final days he may have called out to God.

Someone pointed out that I may be overemphasizing how the way Home to God is through recognizing his love for us. We simply reach out for him. I responded to God's love from the time I was a child and found him to be there for me. It seems to be a theme that appears and reappears in the way I talk, the way I write. That friend's observation pushed me. Just because that was my experience of coming to Christ, doesn't mean everyone has the same one. To the extent that I imply otherwise — it is not right.

Author, Ellis Potter reminds us:

We are each different. I can tell you how and why I came to be a Christian, but you cannot do it that way. You have to do it your own way. You are not me. You are unique. You have to come to God and God has to come to you in a way that you understand intellectually, emotionally, existentially, and morally, in ways that I might not understand. According to the Bible, your relationship to God is like a marriage. Christians often speak of sharing their faith, but I don't believe I can share my faith. I think I can share *the* faith — what is believed by Christians

— but I cannot share *my* faith any more than I can share my marriage. I have a marriage, and I can tell you about it, but I cannot share it with you. I have a faith in Jesus Christ, and I can tell you about it, but I cannot share it with you. You have to have your own. You cannot have it by copying another person, or by inheriting it from your parents or your grandparents. We can say that God has no grandchildren. He only has children. Each one has to come directly to him.

(*Three theories of Everything* by Ellis Potter, p. 106)

Amazing Ways

I BELIEVE HE IS right. Easily, easily, off the top of my head I can tell you about three people who came to Jesus in very different ways. My mother came to belief out of fear of going to hell and the fear that she would have colossally failed her six children by not teaching them the gospel if it was true. What would she say to God when he asked her about her six children?

A friend, who was an undergraduate in college, was on his way to class one day when his bicycle got a flat tire. He was repairing it beside the curb when a member of Campus Crusade for Christ walked past and trapped him into listening to a memorized presentation of the "Four Spiritual Laws." This Crusader was extremely annoying and our friend was in no mood to hear him, but he couldn't get the "Laws" out of his head and later that night, he turned to Christ.

One more: Quentin, a young man we knew back in the day, came to our New Mexico commune, because he had a vision of Jesus. He had been on an acid trip and Jesus spoke to him from the cross. He was deeply moved. Quinton knew nothing about Christianity, but he heard we were Christians and he wanted to become one. I'm not recommending this particular way, just saying…

I'm grateful for the differences and surprising ways people reach out to God to find, there he is, ready to meet us where ever we are, even with our doubts and unanswered questions. God operates unfathomably outside my box. I think this may be the core Gift of Christmas; that Christ was born to bring us an amazing salvation, and he has the power to bring us home in a thousand ways from a thousand places in the wilderness. So I don't care how my grandfather came to God. If he did. I just want him to be there when I die.

In my memoir, *The Exact Place* I included a recipe from Grandma Frolander — Lemon Angel Pie. She often made it for holiday meals. It was always a part of Christmas and it became one of my mother's traditions, too. We looked forward to this light-as-air dessert. There was always room for it even though we were stuffed with mashed potatoes, turkey, gravy, dressing, and cranberries. The lemon pie — intense filling, lightly sandwiched between two layers of whipped cream, resting on a crunchy meringue — is still a favorite dessert. A bite of heaven. Perhaps it will be featured at God's Table? I don't know.

But for now we enjoy this pleasing bite; a taste, perhaps, of a more perfect life — one where we remember to say "I love you." On time. Where death no longer stalks us, because it's been conquered by our Friend and Savior, Jesus. For all time. So, forever and ever may Christmas always be merry to you.

Grandma Frolander's Angel Pie

Meringue Crust:

> 4 egg whites
> ¼ t. cream of tartar
> 1 cup sugar

Beat egg whites and until foamy. Gradually add cream of tartar and sugar, beating until meringue stands in stiff peaks. Spread in a buttered 9-inch pie plate. Or shape into 9 small meringues on a sheet of parchment on a baking sheet. Bake at 275° for one hour or until crust is dry all the way through. Turn oven off. Allow crust to cool in the oven for several hours.

Lemon filling:

4 egg yolks

½ cup sugar

1 lemon, juice and zest

In a saucepan beat yolks until thick. Add sugar and lemon. Stirring constantly, thicken over medium heat.

1 cup cream, whipped, no sugar added.

Spread ½ the whipped cream on top of cooled meringue. Carefully spread lemon filling as the next layer. Spread remaining whipped cream on top of filling. Refrigerate until served.

Notes on Resources

The following are listed in order of their appearance in the book:

Pohl, Christine D., *Making Room: Recovering Hospitality as a Christian Tradition* (Grand Rapids: Eerdmans, 1999).

Graham, Kenneth, *Wind in the Willows* (New York, NY: Holt, Rinehart, & Winston, 1980).

Ashworth, Andi, *Real Love for Real Life: The Art and Work of Caring* (Colorado Springs, CO: Shaw, 2002).

Pipher, Mary, *Another Country: Navigating the Emotional Terrain of our Elders* (New York, NY: Penguin Putnam, 1999).

Oden, Thomas, *The Good Works Reader* (Grand Rapids, MI: Eerdmans, 2007).

Over the Rhine, *Good Dog Bad Dog*, "All I Need is Everything" CD (Independent release, 1996)

Buechner, Frederick, *Wishful Thinking: A Seeker's ABC* (New York, NY: Harper & Row, 1993).

Tolkien, J.R.R., *The Hobbit* (New York, NY: Ballantine, 1966)

Schaeffer, Edith, *Dear Family: The L'Abri Family Letters* (New York, NY: Harper Collins, 1989).

Schaeffer, Edith, *Hidden Art* (Wheaton, IL: Tyndale House, 1971).

Hilfiker, David, "When Mental Illness Blocks the Spirit," online at www.davidhilfiker.com.

Sacks, Oliver, *The Man Who Mistook His Wife for a Hat: and other Clinical Tales* (New York, NY: Summit Books, 1986).

Swinton, John, *Resurrecting the Person: Friendship and care of People with Mental Health Problems* (Nashville, TN: Abingdon Press, 2000).

Johnson, Sue, *Hold Me Tight: Seven Conversations for a Lifetime of Love* (New York, NY: Little, Brown, 2008)

"What the #$*! Do We (K)now!?" Documentary released in 2004.

Smith, Bruce, *Winter Light* (Oro Valley, AZ: Kalos Press, 2011)

Cloud & Townsend, *Boundaries: When to Say Yes, How to Say No to Take Control of Your Life* (Grand Rapids, MI: Zondervan, 1992).

Palmer, Parker, *Let Your Life Speak: Listening for the Voice of Vocation* (San Francisco, CA: Jossey Bass, 1999)

Chesterton, G.K., *Tremendous Trifles* (New York, NY: Dover, 2007).

Doriani, Dan & Collins, Jack, "Rearing Covenant Children in Faith" (Covenant Seminary, 1996).

Powell, Julie, *Julie and Julia: 365 Days, 524 Recipes, 1 Tiny Apartment Kitchen* (New York, NY: Bullfinch Press, 2005).

Claiborne, Wilson-Hartgrove, Okoro, *Common Prayer: A Liturgy for Ordinary Radicals* (Grand Rapids, MI: Zondervan, 2010).

Potter, Ellis, *Three Theories of Everything* (Switzerland: Destinēe S.A., 2012)

Acknowledgements

I am thankful for many great writers whose work represents voices as different from one another as Minnesota is from Hawaii. From Anne Lamott's hilarious memoirs to Cormac McCarthy's minimalist, sometimes violent fiction — I have loved and learned from many. They gave me enough courage to embrace my own voice.

From my heart I salute the readers who loyally followed *Notes From Toad Hall* over the years and the many who responded with notes of their own. Without their encouragement, I would have quit long ago because unlike those who write for the sheer joy of it, I needed to know if we were connecting or not. Thank you for sticking with me.

I am deeply grateful for Andi, Katy and Peggy who kept praying, when in the process of editing these pieces, I saw the accumulated me and was so disheartened I wanted to jump off the project. With patience and kindness you prayed me to safer ground.

I'm grateful for my editor Ed Eubanks, who believed in this project from the beginning and kept us working toward deadlines.

Many thanks to Jeremy Huggins. You have a unique ability to critique and teach with kindness. I don't know how you navigate fragile egos and barely leave a footprint, but I love you for it.

To my dear friend Anita Gorder, your gracious help made it easier to focus knowing supper was on its way on days when I was on a roll and continued writing. Thank you so much.

Thanks to our Board of Directors (the members changed a little over the years) — Steve, Ann, Butch, Greg, Henry, Craig, Maze, Dan, Donald, Bonnie, Ed, and Paul — all of you were glad to have *Notes* as one of the voices that represented Ransom Fellowship.

Ed Hague, thank you for making me think I'm really okay most of the time and for keeping me company when neither of us was okay. For encouraging a pattern of deep growth in Christ despite, or especially in, suffering. For liking what I wrote even when I didn't. Thank you for being present with your wit and sharp opinions even through what may be your final days here on earth. It is a joy to walk with you.

Special thanks to our children, their spouses and our grandchildren. Each of you have given unique gifts in living in the ordinary and the everyday. Without the richness of those experiences I would be barren and poor. I can't imagine life without you. I love you.

Finally, Denis. You have been my most faithful supporter, believing that God calls us and uses us for his glory in spite of ourselves. In the early years when you critiqued my writing, which I insisted I wanted and needed, you persevered in spite of my hostility. There were many times when I thought of giving up because each issue of *Notes* precipitated a crisis, not because of what I wrote about us — you were always a pretty good sport about that — but because I couldn't take the criticism. It took years to agree that I am a writer. The irony of writing about what God was doing in our lives while having a marriage conflict made it difficult to believe I should be writing a ministry newsletter at all. Thank you. Thank you.

About
Margie L. Haack

Margie was born in northern Minnesota just south of the Canadian border. She is co-founder and co-director of Ransom Fellowship along with her husband, Denis. They share a love for home and hospitality, for art and culture, and for the prodigal nature of God's work in ordinary life.

For thirty-three years she published *Notes from Toad Hall*, their ministry's newsletter. She is author of *The Exact Place*, a coming-to-faith memoir and also writes a blog — www.toadsdrinkcoffee. blogspot.com — finding what's funny, what's holy, what's suffering in the everyday.

She and Denis are the parents of three grown children and eight grandchildren which keeps them securely bound to real life.

About
Kalos Press

KALOS PRESS WAS ESTABLISHED to give a voice to literary fiction, memoir, essays, poetry, devotional writing, and Christian Reflection — works of excellent quality, outside of the mainstream Christian publishing industry.

We believe that good writing is beautiful in form and in function, and is capable of being an instrument of transformation. It is our hope and ambition that every title produced by Kalos Press will live up to this belief.

For more information about Kalos Press, *God in the Sink*, and/or our other titles, or for ordering information, visit us on our website: www.kalospress.org, or contact us by e-mail at info@kalospress.org.

Digital Copies Of
God in the Sink

At Kalos Press, we've found that we often appreciate owning both print and digital editions of the books we read; perhaps you have found this as well. In our gratitude to you for purchasing a print version of this book, we are pleased to offer you free copies of the digital editions of *God in the Sink*. To obtain one or more of these, simply visit the eStore of our parent ministry, Doulos Resources (estore.doulosresources.org) and enter the following discount code during checkout:

GodintheSinkDiscount

If you purchased a digital edition, you may use the same discount code to receive a discount deducting the full price of your digital edition off of the purchase price for a print edition. You may also use this discount code to receive $2.00 off of the purchase of Margie's other Kalos Press title, *The Exact Place*.

Thank you for your support!

CPSIA information can be obtained at www.ICGtesting.com
Printed in the USA
LVOW07s1418111214

418340LV00002B/3/P